My Mother

My Mother

Recollections

of

Maternal Influence

John Mitchell

"We will revive those times,, and in our memories
Preserve and still keep fresh, like flowers in water,
Those happy days." - Denham

"My home! the sight of its love is breathing
  In every wind that plays across my track."

Solid Ground Christian Books
Birmingham, Alabama USA

Solid Ground Christian Books
715 Oak Grove Rd
Birmingham, AL 35209
205-443-0311
sgcb@charter.net
http://solid-ground-books.com

MY MOTHER
Recollections of Maternal Influence

John Mitchell (1794-1870)

Solid Ground Classic Reprints

First edition April 2007

Taken from 1855 edition by Gould & Lincoln, Boston, MA

Cover work by Borgo Design, Tuscaloosa, AL
Contact them at nelbrown@comcast.net

Cover image is taken from the frontispiece of the original edition by Gould & Lincoln which is an image of the scene described on page 220 of this edition.

1-59925-071-3

Preface to New Edition

"Honor your father and your mother; that your days may be long upon the land which the LORD your God is giving you" (Exodus 20:12). This book is in fulfillment of this commandment of our Lord.

John Mitchell was a gifted minister of the Gospel who never forgot the woman who was responsible for him being the man he became. He fulfilled another portion of Scripture when he determined to write this tribute: "Her children rise up and call her blessed" (Proverbs 31:28). Every word is dipped in the pen of love, as one man honors the godly woman who brought him into the world, and brought him up to serve God.

I have known about this book for a few years, but I was not able to find a copy to purchase. I was drawn by the simple title: *My Mother*. I was also drawn by the numerous commendations I read about the usefulness of this volume. When the Lord provided me with an opportunity to acquire this book I did so with great anticipation. I was not disappointed when I finally opened these pages to read the words of tribute by a grateful son.

Solid Ground Christian Books is delighted to have this book brought back into print in time for Mother's Day 2007. We are fully committed to honor motherhood in a day that women are under constant pressure to seek their identity outside the home. Our very first book, which was published six years ago, was *Mothers of the Wise and Good*. What a joy to be able to bring forth this treasure to encourage mothers to lay down their lives for their children. May the Lord bless this reprint to the glory of His name and the good of His people.

Michael Gaydosh
Solid Ground Christian Books

PUBLISHERS' ADVERTISEMENT.

THIS work was originally published in 1849. It speedily ran through three editions, when the failure of its publisher arrested its further success. What copies remained on sale were soon bought up, and the work, for a time, disappeared from the market.

It is now presented to the public with the essential claims of a new work. This is done at the urgent solicitation of those whose knowledge of the book and whose literary judgment entitle them to speak with authority in the matter. To them it seemed to be a work so singularly charming in its whole character, and in all its details, that they would not willingly let it die. "It is one of those rare pictures," writes one who is himself an author of celebrity, "painted from life with the exquisite skill of one of the old masters, which so seldom present themselves to the amateur." The present publishers have undertaken its republication in the full confidence that the reading public will endorse this judgment.

In regard to the aim and character of the work, the author says, in a recent communication, that, "however much of a biographical nature may be found in it, it was not intended as a biography, as some have conceived it to have been. Its aim was *educational*. It was believed that such observations on maternal influence and domestic life as are here drawn from memory, presented in a narrative way, might be attractive and useful to mothers of young families; perhaps, also, to husbands and fathers."

The author, who has already distinguished himself in other walks of literature, chooses for the present to conceal his name; the time may come when the veil will be removed. His motives for publishing the book anonymously will be appreciated and honored by every person of due sensibility. "Involving, as it does," he writes, "so much that is of a personal nature, I never could have written it except under cover of assumed names or blanks. Indeed, I was almost conscience-stricken, when I had done it, for having written so much, even anonymously, concerning a venerated parent, while she was living, without her knowledge and consent; and was at a loss how to justify myself to her, except by a plea always powerful with her — *the hope of accomplishing some good by it*, with, at the same time, a studious concealment of places and persons. There were others, also, whose humility in some cases, or whose pride or love of kindred in others, might be hurt, if they were named, or palpably or traceably alluded to."

The present edition contains an additional chapter of new matter, that essentially enhances its value.

GOULD AND LINCOLN.

PREFACE.

This volume needs no other preface than the following note:—

My Dear Mrs. ——:

I have, as you perceive, complied with your request—more at length, and more discursively than I intended, or you, perhaps, expected or desired. You wanted some account of my mother *as* a mother, and I have given you here a miscellany of characters, incidents, reflections, and I know not what. The history of the mother, as such, is, so far as domestic education is concerned, almost necessarily the history of the family itself.

The freedom I have felt in writing to a friend, or my filial partialities, or that fondness we all naturally have for dwelling on remembered scenes, especially those of our childhood, when once we get among them, any one or all of these things may have been the cause of my responding to your request with so copious a manuscript.

It is not necessary that I should say to you that, in these notices of a beloved parent, there is nothing very novel or extraordinary. They exhibit only a plain

PREFACE.

Christian woman bringing up a family under certain circumstances, more or less peculiar, but only so as the circumstances of every family are different from those of every other. It is the wisdom and experience of such as are in the ordinary walks of life that are most likely to be useful. For the histories of those whose circumstances have been extraordinary, who have moved in higher spheres than others, or have run through rare adventures, are presented to us as unique or extreme cases; which, though they are more entertaining, are less available for common use.

If these humble reminiscences prove of any service to you, as I hope they may, in the discharge of your own responsible duties as a mother; if they in some measure justify the confidence expressed by you, that you will "gather wisdom from her methods, and fidelity and courage from her faith, patience, and success," I shall not regret the hours spent in writing them.

Wishing you all needed wisdom, and much happiness in the successful training of your young and hopeful charge, I remain,

Your friend and Christian brother,

CONTENTS.

PREFACE.

Note addressed to a Lady, ... iii.

CHAPTER I.

My Mother's Ancestry.—Home of her Childhood.—The Revolution.—Death of a Sister.—Presentiment.—My Mother's Conversion, ... 9

CHAPTER II.

My Mother's Marriage.—The Young Wife leaving Home and Kindred.—New Relations and New Influences.—Her Husband's Family.—Her Father-in-law, . . . 19

CHAPTER III.

An Emigrant Family.—Bereaved of its Head.—Agnes Buchanan.—Old French War.—Character and Influence of my Grandfather.—Father and Son.—Our Homestead.—My Grandmother, ... 26

CHAPTER IV.

Seed Sown in the Morning.—Pest-house.—Aunt Rumah. Suspension of Maternal Care.—Ground Lost, . . 38

CHAPTER V.

Growing Solicitude.—Great Ends of Domestic Education.—Physical Education.—Mental Culture.—Littlepark Castle.—Opposing Influence, ... 53

CONTENTS.

CHAPTER VI.

Religious Culture.—Temporal Prosperity.—Work-people.—
Michael Bruin. —Spirit-Drinking, ... 62

CHAPTER VII.

Conflicting Views and Agencies.—The Principal Thing.—
Power of Meekness.—Mischief-maker.—Unsustained Endeavors.—Importance of a Father's Aid.—Influence of
Domestic Worship.—Moral Heroism, ... 74

CHAPTER VIII.

Hope Deferred.—Susan's Marriage.—Fire.—Sickness.—
Conversion.—Afflictions Sanctified.—Conversion.—Incident.—Prediction.—At College.—Installation.—Conversion, ... 90

CHAPTER IX.

My Father.—His Moral Character.—Moral Idiosyncrasies.
—Sympathetic Religion.—Death of my Grandfather, . 104

CHAPTER X.

Pecuniary Losses and Embarrassments.—An Over-cast Sky.
—Calamities Protracted.—Home.—Morality of the Endorsing System, ... 115

CHAPTER XI.

The Day of Adversity.—Christian Counsel.—My Father.—
His Complicated Troubles.—Desponding Fears for his
Spiritual State.—Concert of Prayer.—A Night of Intercession.—Earnest Appeal and Proposal.—My Father's
Conversion.—Public Profession.—Family Prayer.—My
Father's Death.—Descent of Character in Families, 131

CONTENTS.

CHAPTER XII.

Educational Views and Methods.—The Christian Plan, . 151

CHAPTER XIII.

Parental Government.— Offending Chair.— Parental Instinct, ... 155

CHAPTER XIV.

Respect to Parents.—History of an Undutiful Son.—Unnatural Children.—Affectionate Granddaughter.—Sin Punished.—Dutifulness Rewarded.— Fraternal Love.— Respect to Age, ... 166

CHAPTER XV.

Discrimination with respect to the Faults of Children.—Beehive.—Injustice to the Feelings and Behavior of Children.—Mrs. Howitt's Elephant.—Plea for Little People.—Children's Perception of Things, ... 177

CHAPTER XVI.

Restraint and Freedom.—Effects of Excessive Supervision.—Wholesome Neglect.—My Mother's Course.—Attempt at Reaping.—Moral Care.—Companionships.—An Isolated Family.—Acquaintance with the World, . . . 188

CHAPTER XVII.

Commendation and Reproof.—Love of Approbation.—A Mother's Gift.—A Mother's Kiss, ... 202

CHAPTER XVIII.

Young Life in the Country.—Physical Education of Girls.—My Sisters.—Young Ladies on Horseback.—Apple Gathering.—Aeropathy.—Our Climate, . . . 203

CONTENTS.

CHAPTER XIX.

Constancy of Teaching and Impression.—Habitual Reference to the Bible.—Lessons from the Living World.—Society of the Good.—Nature and its Teachings.—The Flower Garden.—The Book of Providence, . . 216

CHAPTER XX.

Educational uses of Employment.—Practical Benevolence.—Incidents in Edinburgh.—Moral Influence of Love of Home.—Matrimony.—Religious Character of my Mother.—Filial Regrets.—Passion for the Sea.—Concluding Paragraphs, ... 226

CHAPTER XXI.

The Old Homestead Revisited.—A Boy's Resolve.—Changes.—The Old Meeting-house.—Adventure on the River.—Trusting in Providence.—The Bethel Oak.—Bruin.—The Shady Mile.—Farewell.—Bruin's Death, ... 241

MY MOTHER.

CHAPTER I.

My Mother's Ancestry.—Home of her Childhood.—The Revolution.—Death of a Sister.—My Mother's Conversion.

My mother's earliest American progenitors sleep with the Pilgrim settlers of Saybrook. From thence her grandparents removed to the town of her nativity; to which they gave the name of one of the western cities of England, from which the family emigrated.

The house in which she was born, above eighty years ago, was among the most endeared and venerated objects of my regard in childhood ; and my memory still recalls it as a picture of the age in which, and a memorial of the family by whom, it was erected. It was a large and lofty mansion, on a rising ground, with fine prospects; ancient, *very* ancient, as it seemed to me, dating three generations back of mine!—which, in a child's mind, is as venerable an antiquity almost as that of the Hebrew patriarchs. Its generous dimensions, huge timbers, and vast chimney, might remind one of the leading idea of the Pilgrims, who felt, in every thing, that they were laying foundations, and building for posterity. It was somewhat elaborately ornamented after the fashion of its day: the two-leaved front door, and the windows, were adorned with scrolls and rosettes; the cornice was Corinthian; the parlors wainscoted; with ceilings composed of the flooring above, planed, matched, and laid on beaded chestnut sleepers; the hearths of fine red sandstone edged round with raised mouldings— very inconvenient to the maids that swept them. The well-gear was of that primitive sort that shows so well in a picture, and *sings* so well in that song of the "Old oaken bucket that hangs in the well"—to wit, the crotch, sweep, and pole. Convenient to the well was what they called a *wash-stone*, being a rough-hewn, or rusticated sand-stone block, nicely hollowed out for a wash-basin, where the men, coming from the fields, washed. We children, when we visited our grandparents, amused ourselves with washing in it, on a fragrant morning, beneath the rose-tree that hung profusely over it. A single tree stood before the house—more venerable than it—a lofty, wide-spreading white-oak, of the primeval forest, spared by the builders of the house, dateless in the memory of man. I would go a long way now to lie down in its shade, or gather acorns under it, as I used to do; but when the house was taken down, a sacrilegious axe felled the tree also, though it was still as vigorous as it was a century, it may be many centuries, before.

The neighborhood and parish in which the old house stood, and was conspicuous in its day, was of a peculiarly primitive and rural character. There were small clusters of houses here and there, and single habitations scattered along quiet winding roads, none of which were elegant, but all respectable and comfortable, with a soil just sufficiently fertile to secure both industry and contentment, and put the occupants into that medium condition for which the son of Jakeh prayed.

How peaceful, to look at it, was that rural, amiable neighborhood! and yet it was disquieted, in that olden time to which this history here refers, by the rude alarms of war. My mother was in her eighth year when the startling news came of the skirmishing at Lexington, followed by the still more exciting battle of Bunker Hill. Thenceforward her childhood was a season of anxiety. Her father, then in the prime of life, partook of the patriotic enthusiasm of the time, and, with a captain's commission, leaving his plough in the furrow, like Putnam, immediately raised a company of men, and drilled them on a small common in front of his house. Many a time have I played on that little plat, with the children of the place, regarding the ground with deep historic interest, from its association with him and his patriotic band. It was with me one of the high-places of the Revolution.

They were soon summoned to the camp. I seem to hear them as they march away, with fife and drum, every wife and mother's, every child's ear, listening to the fainter-growing sound. Then, till the war was ended, how many rumors, confirmed and unconfirmed, came to agitate the hearts that had their home among those sweet hills and valleys! Once, in one or two weeks, there passed along that rural old road, up and down, a man on horseback, with saddle-bags, in character of post-rider, whose arrival, at one little office and another, was expected with far deeper interest than is that of the mail-loaded Atlantic steamer now, at our city wharves. Often the tidings he brought clothed a family in mourning.

As my grandmother was the wife of the captain of the company gone from there, it was natural that people should resort to her for the latest and fullest information from the war; and being an amiable and Christian woman, it was the more to be expected that such as lost friends, whether by the sword or by sickness, should resort to her for consolation. They would beg her to tell them, if possible, the minutest particulars of the catastrophe or sickness of the husband, son, or brother whom they deplored. And so the good lady's four children—of whom Abigail, my mother, was the third—were kept in continual excitement. They had a father, and she a husband, at the place whence these eventful rumors came; they were, therefore, in circumstances to feel the liveliest sympathy with others, as well as to feel on their own account. What others felt or apprehended, they felt and apprehended. Every light and shadow of the time fell on them.

However, they got inured to this; and like the

soldiers in the field, not only wives and mothers, but even their young daughters, imbibed the calm and lofty heroism of the day, and, trusting in God, laid aside at length their agitating fears. My mother, naturally of a somewhat energetic character, experienced then, at that tender age, a discipline of mind and heart which was visible in her ever after : resolute, patient, magnanimous, sympathizing—a genuine daughter of '76.

Captain W., her father, who was a good officer as well as a devoted patriot, was in some of the greatest scenes and crises of the war, losing a large per centage of his men, but surviving himself to witness and enjoy, to a good old age, the liberty he had contributed to achieve. He was a man of singular purity of manners—unworthy else of the Revolution and the age. His gentlemanly character, as well as the amiable manners of his wife, made his house to be much resorted to by intelligent and good people. This, when means for a superior education were rare and difficult to reach, was a great advantage to their children. How frequently, and justly, do old people exclaim at the comparative advantages of children now ! My mother received no other schooling than what she had at the very ordinary parish school. Books then were rare, children's books especially. But whether that dearth, or the present surfeit, were the greater evil, admits, perhaps, of question. If they read less then than we do now, they reflected more; they read the Bible more; and parents trusted less to books, and more to their own personal endeavors, to form the minds and manners of their children.

A providence occurred in the early history of the family which made a tender and enduring impression on my mother's mind: it was the death of her eldest sister, in the twelfth year of her age. The character of the child, and the circumstances of her death, gave a more than ordinary interest to her memory. She possessed an intelligent and thoughtful mind, and a heart large and finely sympathetic. Some time before her death, though in apparent health, she became affected with a presentiment of that event. Her mother endeavored to turn her from such an impression, representing it as imaginary, and almost criminal, but in vain. The child was silent to her reasonings, but her pensiveness remained. Returning from school one evening, she resumed an unfinished piece of sewing, and worked at it till the light was so far gone that her mother feared she would injure her eyes; but she begged permission to finish it. "It is almost done, mother, and if I do not finish it now, I never shall." She finished it, folded it up, and laid it away. It was the last work she ever did. In the morning there was a flush on her cheek; she had a fever, grew worse, and, in less than a week, died; expressing in the final hour, with Christian resignation, and a sweet smile, a distinct and most affectionate adieu to each one of the family, to her mother last of all. There seemed to be something marked in her look and manner toward her mother (of whom she was exceedingly fond), as if she had said—You see I was not mistaken; it was *not* an unfounded imagination; I heard a voice you could not hear; it calls me now; adieu, till I see you in heaven!

I have not much faith in such presentiments; they are generally, if not always, purely imaginary —the effect of a morbid condition of body or mind, unwarranted by Scripture and seldom justified by the event.

In the case before us, I state the facts, and leave you to dispose of them as you please. The bereavement—I do not say the presentiment—was a providence not lost upon the survivors, particularly upon Abigail. While she mourned for her beloved sister, she could not bear that the separation should be endless. To think of her was to think of heaven; and to think of heaven was to weaken her attachment to this world. How often are the sorrows of childhood the saving of the soul!

It was not, however, till at about the age of seventeen, that my mother became the subject of deep and decisive religious impressions. With the great question she was exercised for months— reading her Bible, praying, with an ear open to every word that fell from Christian lips, but keeping her feelings in a great degree to herself. She seemed to herself to be alone in this inquiry; there was no special religious interest around her; the young were thoughtless, the old were worldly; even Christians appeared to be settled on their lees. Such was the state of things too generally in the country during, and subsequently to, the Revolution. The war absorbed all thought and feeling while it lasted, and then liberty, commerce, and unwonted thrift followed, with intoxicating effect.

She found peace, at length—the peace of God which passeth knowledge. From that time onward she was an unwavering, happy follower of Christ, proving by a life of faith and patience that the religion of her youth was no shallow sentiment, or superficial garb.

God leads the blind by a way they know not. He takes his own time, as well as his own method, to mature his preparatory work. Perhaps those many months of anxious, unrelieved, *lone* inquiry, and those previous years of less deep, fluctuating, but never ceasing concern, were intended to work a more absolute decision in her eventually, and so to prepare her to withstand the wordly influences to which, in new relations, she was ere long to be exposed.

CHAPTER II.

My Mother's Marriage.—The young Wife leaving her Home and Kindred.
—Her Father-in-law.

My mother was married at the age of twenty-one. She did not leave her parental home without regrets deep and tender, happy as she was in the home of her adoption. Nor were the regrets of those she left less than hers; for she had been an affectionate and helpful daughter, and a fond sister. And, indeed, the removal of a daughter and sister, going out thus from her native home to be no more an inmate there; to be the subject of new relations and endearments even more intimate and tender than those she leaves behind; to take upon her new responsibilities and cares, and to be involved, for better or for worse, in other fortunes than those which heretofore have concerned her, does produce a mingled feeling of sympathy and bereavement almost funereal. Smiles and congratulations are the prevailing expression at weddings, and they should be so; yet there are tears mingled with the smiles, and who can censure them, or say they are out of place? The Bible, that acquaints itself with every human feeling, and more than all with the affections and sympathies of domestic life, has not omitted scenes like this. What regret does the family of Bethuel feel at "sending away" Rebekah. They give their consent to her going as being the will of God, believing that that match at least was made in heaven. "The thing proceedeth from the Lord," said they; "we cannot speak to thee good or bad." Nor did they doubt that the gain was greater than the sacrifice. Yet, feeling what a chasm was about to be made in their little world, they inclined to detain her awhile. "Let the damsel abide with us a few days, at the least ten; after that she shall go." That is, we consent if she does; it shall be no reluctant match. "We will call the damsel, and inquire at her mouth. And they called Rebekah, and said unto her, Wilt thou go with this man? And she said, I will go. And they sent away Rebekah, and her nurse, and Abraham's servant, and his men."

My father, three years older than my mother, was of the same parish, having his home a couple of miles from hers. He was strong and well made, with a ruddy complexion, blue eyes, and thick, dark, wavy hair. She also was symmetrically formed, and had a fine healthy complexion. The expression of her face, ordinarily, was that of cheerful and thoughtful serenity, but it was very susceptible to emotion. His education, so far as letters were concerned, was superior to hers, and to that of most of the young men about him, he having enjoyed, to some extent, the best advantages the time afforded, short of college. He was not a professor of religion, though of blameless morals and amiable disposition. He was an only son, and had an only sister, a beautiful and sprightly girl.

You requested me to give you the history of a mother rearing a family: in order to do so, it is necessary to acquaint you with the leading circumstances, propitious and unpropitious, by which her maternal labors were attended. You need especially to know something of the character of those with whose views and interests she comes most immediately and intimately into contact. When a young wife leaves the society of her own kindred, and goes to reside among those of her husband, she passes under a new set of influences, favorable or unfavorable to her character and wishes. If she finds their sentiments harmonious with her own, and if both are elevated and refined, then the union is the augmented flow of a bright and tranquil stream. More happy still for her, if superior worth, or social standing, on their part, affords a welcome influence to lift her to their level. But often she becomes allied to those whose views and ways are quite diverse from hers. The two families, or races, have been trained on different systems, trained to different habits, prejudices, and aims. Then, supposing their standard to be inferior to hers, it will usually, and almost necessarily happen, either that she will elevate them, or they depress her. Especially must this ensue with regard to the parties most intimately related and concerned—the husband and wife. And it requires great force and constancy of character on her part, or on his, as the case may be, to escape the worse and secure the better issue. Hence, in such a connection, of how much deeper consideration is the question of *family*—I mean in the social and moral sense—than the question of wealth or rank! If I ally myself to sordid, or coarse, or worldly minds, and oblige myself to intimacy with them, and to mix my race with theirs, as I do by marriage, there are no external advantages of wealth or standing that can balance the evil, to me or to my children, not even if wealth and distinction were permanent, which cannot be expected. Estates melt away, and names—*all* names, but those of virtue and of goodness—fade, and are destined to fade, and be forgotten; but the *race* lives on; its inherited and still inherent characteristics descend to the future with it, and become the inheritance and the blight of my own posterity. There are races with which I would not mix myself and my posterity for all the wealth and rank of the proudest family on earth.

I do by no means say these things to intimate the character of the family into which my mother married. In intelligence and social standing, they were equal to hers; in wealth, superior. Their reputation in a moral point of view was unblemished; they had many desirable qualities. But while she and most of her kindred were pious, they and most of theirs were wholly worldly. And that worldliness was the ungenial atmosphere in which she was obliged to live, and bring up her children. If it did not engender direct opposition, 't did occasion the absence of all sympathy, on their part, with her religious views and endeavors. She was isolated in it, to say no worse. Its influence, however, was more than negative: it opposed and defeated much that she proposed, and ardently wished to effect, for the intellectual as well as the spiritual benefit of her children. And I may as well mention here a particular influence, more embarrassing than any other, which she encountered from the first, in the character of her father-in-law.

He was a man of great energy and thrift, and every one about him felt his sway. Over his son especially, he maintained an almost absolute— I do not say an arbitrary, but yet an almost absolute—ascendency; and he sought to extend the same over the daughter-in-law, and over their children. And being entirely worldly in his views, it required great firmness, and much meekness of wisdom, on the part of our mother to withstand it as to herself, and to neutralize its effect upon her family, so far as it might be prejudicial to their spiritual well-being.

It will be pertinent to our purpose to give an

outline of his history, and the more so, as it will bring to our notice *another* mother, but for whose remote but hallowed influence the complexion of our own religious history might have been quite different from what it has been. To that subject, therefore, I shall devote the following chapter.

CHAPTER III.

An Emigrant Family.—Bereaved of its Head.—Agnes Buchanan.—Old French War.—Character and Influence of my Grandfather.—His Wife.

The parents of my grandfather emigrated hither from Scotland, in 1755. They were respectable and worthy people. Within a few months after their arrival, the husband died, leaving the widow with several daughters, and one son, the subject of this notice, who was then about seventeen years old. Besides the cost of emigration, greater then than now, they had met with losses, and the family were left in very slender circumstances. Bereaved, destitute, in a land of strangers, with a group of dependent children about her, the case of the widow seemed desolate enough.

But she was a woman of great faith. Hers was the widow's God, and theirs the Father of the fatherless, and on him she stayed herself. The death of her husband did not occasion the discontinuance of their family devotions; she took that duty on herself. Morning and evening, with her children, she read the Scriptures, and offered up prayer to Him whose support and blessing they so manifestly needed. AGNES BUCHANAN was her maiden name. I was told by the late venerable Judge ——, who was her nephew, that she was of the same stock as Dr. Claudius Buchanan, being great aunt, I think, to that excellent and distinguished man. An admirable woman. I, of course, never knew her; but her memory is sacred to me : for to her faith and prayers, as one interested in the "covenants of promise," I feel myself, as one of her descendants, to be much indebted.

She lived to be eighty-five. Aged people, who remembered her, told me she was one of the most pious and venerable women they ever knew. All her daughters became pious in their youth. And the son also, as I learned from him in his last days, was the subject of deep religious convictions, and of religious light and joy also, as he thought at the time; but, alas! those good beginnings were all swept away and lost by the tide of evil influences that subsequently attended him.

At the time of their arrival in the country, the war with the French in Canada—the Old French War, as we call it—was carried on, and heavy drafts were making on the colonies for that destructive service. Meantime, the young man, my grandfather, arriving at the military age, was enrolled accordingly; and an order coming to the place for its quota of men, he received a private intimation that, by some unrighteous shuffling on the part of those who managed the levy, his name would be reported as one of the drafted. He was a stranger, young, and friendless; there were none to assert or vindicate his rights; and by taking him, the conscription would be so much lighter to the native inhabitants. Whether such unrighteousness was actually meditated, I do not know; but such was his information and his fear; and there certainly was a great temptation to it on the part of those whose sons or brothers were liable to be taken. For that war, waged, as you know, by the ruthless French and their savage allies on the one side, and conducted on the other —for several campaigns at least, till Pitt and Wolfe appeared—by miserably imbecile British generals, was extremely hazardous and fatiguing.

Here, then, was a new distress to the afflicted mother. To say nothing of the perils and the *morals* of the army, how could a family situated as hers was, spare its only son and brother? But there seemed no help for it.

To escape an unfair draft, however, he hastened away, and enlisted in what was called the *team service*. You know that a large number of teams were employed to transport provisions, and other effects, up through the wilderness, to the camps and posts of the army in the north, where we now go by canals and steam. This was a service hardly less perilous—perhaps it was even more perilous and more fatiguing—than that of the army itself. However, it was a choice of evils, and being a *choice*, a voluntary act, it had the name and quality of freedom, and not of slavery—a difference which not only every human will, but every human *muscle* feels; which makes the heaviest task under the one condition lighter than the lightest of the other—say what you will of the blessedness of slavery in any possible form that can be given it. The team service was the forestalling of an oppressive act, real or imaginary; it offered also better wages, and perhaps an earlier discharge.

Into that service, therefore, the young man entered; and in it he experienced as various and rare adventures as a writer of romance might desire, to furnish incident for a volume—sleeping under huge snow-drifts that fell on him in the night, bewildered in dark forests, ambushed by Indians, with all manner of hardships and escapes.

Being a youth of great energy, he attracted the notice of a military commander, and was offered an ensign's commission. In this new capacity he discharged his duty well, saw considerable service, and was promoted.

At the end of the war he returned home, married, and engaging in commerce, as well as agriculture, became a thriving man.

But all this eventful military life, and worldly thrift, effaced, in a very lamentable degree, the impressions of his religious education. Yet he was not immoral, nor skeptical. I am not aware that he ever uttered a word against religion, or a sneer at its professors. So far, the restraints of his education held him throughout life. He was, however, a pretty habitual neglecter of public worship, and, I presume, of his Bible and the closet.

Such was the early history of my Scottish grandsire; such the circumstances that formed his character. I will now describe him as my own earliest recollections present him to me.

He was then somewhat over sixty. He was six feet high and more, perfectly well formed, of great strength, temperate almost to abstemiousness, prompt and active in his movements, with a cheerful manner, a somewhat military air, and a bugle voice that made the hills echo, when he chose to exert it. His dress, always neat and simple, was of a primitive, or at least by-gone and somewhat aristocratic style. In fine, his personal appearance was every way commanding. He was sagacious and far-sighted, and was as independent in his judgments and purposes as he was in his circumstances. I will not say he was of an arbitrary temper, but he was accustomed to direct and control; and there is a kind of decisive supervision over men and things resulting from mere energy of character, that is in effect equivalent to the action of an arbitrary temper; less annoying to the *pride* of its subordinates, but equally preclusive of the spontaneous action of the will. His energy and influence so pervaded every operation and department of his affairs, and of my father's also, that little room was left for any one's will or wisdom to act except his own.

Under such a supervision my father had been formed. Accustomed from his infancy to defer every thing to his father, the same deference was expected and yielded after his majority and marriage. And this explains *his* character in some respects, and goes far to account for, and to excuse, the indiscretions he committed, in a financial way, when, upon his father's death, he came to manage for himself. It is best for young men, generally, to be of age when they *are* of age—I do not say *before*, as they incline to be; for though you keep them under tutelage till they are forty, yet the day of their majority must come at length, and when it does come, will bring with it none the fewer marks of inexperience for the postponement. Indeed, a minority of the judgment and the will extended to forty years or more, establishes such a *habit* of dependence as makes the man more unfit for self-direction than is the youth of twenty-one. In my father's case, the evil was the greater, as he was naturally facile, and needed to have been thrown as early and as much as possible on his own judgment and force of character.

The deference I am speaking of was a habit with him, an educated feeling, which years not abated, but increased; and it was also, in his circumstances, a matter of *necessity*. For the interests of the father and the son were, to a great extent, a blended one: their houses were near each other, being both on the same ample and undivided homestead; their work went on in common, pretty much; and the deeds were all in the father's name: so that there was dependence in fact as well as in feeling. "And the *heir*, as long as he is a child," says the Scripture, "differeth nothing from a servant, though he is lord of all; but is under tutors and governors until the time appointed by the father;" which time is, in many instances, deferred as long as the father lives.

It would have been well if my grandmother's manner with her son had had a tendency to counteract the evil; but instead of this, she, in her fondness, would suffer him to do nothing for himself, and in his own way, if she could help it.

Now, I do not mean to represent my father as a feeble character; quite the contrary. He had a good mind naturally; was fond of reading, and was well informed; nor was there any approximation to effeminacy in his habits. But how often do men of even very superior intellects and attainments fail in the practical details of life. My father's great deficiency was that want of self-reliance, and of that cautious faith in men, without which a man is not qualified to act, judiciously and safely, in an independent, rather than in a subordinate capacity. Hence those embarrassments he brought upon himself and family, of which I shall have to speak farther on. This want was, in him, perhaps, a constitutional one, the fault of an amiable, but too confiding temper; which made it so much the more important to correct it by early discipline. My grandfather was aware of its existence; lamented it; vexed himself about it; foresaw its consequences; but did every thing to aggravate, instead of correcting it. He would hardly suffer him to act with entire independence in the smallest matter; and yet the time was coming when, with his sister, he must leave him to act as administrator and heir to a large estate. He did not fear that he would waste it in prodigal expenditures, or in visionary schemes, but apprehended that he would lose it by mismanagement. What a "vexation of spirit" was such a prospect to such a man! It marred all the happiness he otherwise felt in his great prosperity. This was often apparent in his temper, and not unfrequently expressed itself in words. Having bought a piece of wild land, he took his son with him to see it. It lay in the midst of an extensive forest. "We shall never be able to find it," said the son. "The *officer* will find it, when I am gone," replied the father. Ah! of how many a father, toiling to build up an estate and a name to go down to his posterity, has the wise man described the chagrin, while he thinks of his heirs making shipwreck of his scheme! "Yea, I hated all my labor which I had taken under the sun: because I should leave it to the man that shall be after me. And who knoweth whether he shall be a wise man or a fool? yet shall he have rule over all my labor in which I have labored, and in which I have shown myself wise under the sun."

My grandfather, at the date above mentioned, that of my early recollection of him, had relinquished all personal attention to business, except merely to oversee his farming operations, and look after his investments. He had added field to field, till, for a New England man, his landed property was extensive. That which formed his homestead, including ours, was bounded by a line of some five miles in circuit, and was a picturesque and productive tract. I shall never see another with meadows as green and fragrant, woods as majestic, and waters as sparkling; nor a landscape equally animated with flocks, birds, and cheerful laboring men; which you will easily believe, for I saw these pleasing objects with the eyes of a child, and in the presence of my home.

He used, in summer, to sit in his front door, with his long pipe, and democratic newspaper, and observe the men at work in the fields beneath his eye, his house being on elevated ground; while his horse was always at the door, ready to take him to any part of his domain where his presence might be wanted to give directions, or stimulate his work-people. Many a time have I run the length of a lane, or across a field, to open a gate, or let down bars for him. He would get more work out of his men than other men could; and yet they loved to work for him: for he gave them good cheer, commended their industry, and paid them promptly; and—which always abates the irksomeness of service—they felt that they were serving a superior man. They called him the "Scotch king."

As to his wife, my grandmother, a brief description of her shall suffice. She was as little religious as he, except that she oftener attended public worship; perhaps she was as worldly. But she was of a very different temperament. Her kindness to animals was remarkable. A dozen well-fed cats purred about her, which were suffered to live because she hated to have them killed; out of doors she was beleaguered with her poultry. She would call in children from the street, to give them bread-and-butter. She had good sense naturally, but was wholly unintellectual in her habits, thinking little, and reading less; laughing seldom, but heartily when she did, and generally with good reason. There is often good sense in laughter, as there is often, also, the want of it. She was industriously inclined, but was too fleshy to be active, and so spent most of her time in her chair, knitting and falling asleep. I remember her with affection, for her relationship to us, for her fondness, and her good bits.

Their housekeeper, Deborah, was a character it may concern us to notice; but I will not do it here.

CHAPTER IV.

Pest-house.—Aunt Rumah.—Suspension of Maternal Care.

I HAVE given you the foregoing details, because they concern the subject of these communications. I need not occupy you with a very particular cotemporaneous description of our own family. We were a group of healthy, happy children. Older than myself were Susan and Walter, and younger, Alice, Maria, and Agnes—names always pleasant to me for their sakes. Our mother was early in her endeavors with us, in the way of instruction and impression. "In the morning sow thy seed," was her maxim. Infancy and early childhood are peculiarly the time of the mother's power. As we get older, and grow out of hand, other and disturbing agencies come in to interfere with hers: we come in contact with the world, and are more susceptible to its corrupting power. Then, if the good seed has not been sown already, and with diligence, it finds the ground preoccupied with tares. It was well, in the case of her first children, that she was thus early with us, and that she had already, while we were very young, made impressions on us not easy to be effaced; for a calamity occurred that suspended her maternal care for two years and more.

A physician opened in the place a hospital for patients with the small-pox; a *pest-house* they called it, and a pest it truly was. The small-pox, as every body knows, was formerly a terrible scourge. A single case of it, in city or country, filled the surrounding population with alarm. Chains and fences were thrown across the streets and ways that led to its locality; yet such preventives could not obstruct the winds that bore the contagion on their breath. The only tolerable precaution, and that a hazardous one, was to anticipate it by inoculation; in which form it was safer than in the "natural way." Hence, up to the beginning of the present century, pest-houses were a part of the sanitary history of each successive generation. Now, we merely scratch an infant's arm, and insert a little vaccine matter, which in its effects scarcely occasions the least uneasiness to babe or nurse, and there is its panoply against the terrible invader. In how many ways is the world improving, both physically and morally!

It was strange news to us children, that we were to exchange our pleasant home for the pest-house, and still more strange, that the three eldest of us were to go without our parents. It being not convenient for all to go at once, it was arranged that we should go first, and then our mother with the remaining three. Our father had been inoculated many years before, and was not to go.

To the pest-house, therefore, we were taken, Susan, Walter, and myself, being committed to the care of a woman who accompanied us. I well remember our little history there. The house was an old, forlorn thing, in a wild, outlandish place; lone, dark, comfortless, surrounded by a half-cleared forest, with only a by-road leading to it. Over it hung a dull white flag. Within were all sorts of people, old and young. Some of them, especially some rude young men, were full of mirth and noise. But their levity soon abated when they saw the disease assuming a formidable aspect in the case of some. I shall never forget the appearance of one young man as he sat bolstered up in an arm-chair, the face, hands, bosom, every visible part of him covered with loathsome pustules. He died; and so did one or two others; and were laid in their graves by star-light.

As for us, we had the disease lightly enough. But they almost starved us with the prescribed diet of water-gruel, without salt, and bread and water. It was no great hardship that they made us sleep on hard straw-beds, winter though it was; but to have no bedstead but the floor, with a dozen other sleepers in the same apartment, was not so agreeable.

The woman, Miss Rumah, to whom we were intrusted, was of a peevish temper, and added little to our comfort. She was, I am sorry to say, a maiden cousin of our father's. However, we contrived to pass our time tolerably—for children are full of expedients: we roamed about in fair weather as far as the limits permitted; we searched for nuts, if the ground was bare, but the squirrels had preceded us; and for myself, when nothing better offered, I rolled up snow-balls. I was thus employed, as I remember, when I began to be conscious of strange sensations coming over me; I felt ill; my head ached; the air was cold and raw;

the snow-clad earth looked dismal, and I went into the no less dismal house. There was no one there to whom I cared to say I was sick, none whose sympathy I looked for, my sister and brother excepted; but my illness was apparent, and they said I had the "symptoms." I was that day six years old.

Our father came daily to see us, and glad we were. Our mother could not come to the house on account of the exposure; but she came as often as she could (the distance being considerable) as far as the stone wall which formed our limits on that side, and would deposit on it parched corn, or some other little article not prohibited by our regimen; but when we ran toward her, she was obliged to retire precipitately beyond speaking distance.

When we were ready to be discharged, our father came to take us away, bringing our mother and three little sisters to take our places. At home we underwent the necessary ablutions and changes of apparel, and then were at liberty to run about and enjoy again our wonted play-places and pastimes. But it did not seem like home: our mother was not there. And in her place, as housekeeper, was the same woman of whose gentle care we had already had experience at the house with the dull white flag. Miss Rumah had no love for children. We soon found her dynasty uncomfortable, even more so than at the pest-house, for there she had fewer cares and more observers. Under our mother's eye, we had been accustomed to all innocent liberties, as well as to all wholesome restraints; but with Miss Rumah it was all restraint, and no liberty. We could not *stir* without disturbing her. "Hush! there." "I'll have you all down cellar." "What a racket!" "There, you mischief!" Many such rebukes, with unpleasant names and epithets, our unaccustomed ears had to endure. "Monstrous regimen of women."

Our mother and the little ones were staying longer than we had done; it seemed as if they never would come home. Our father, who went daily to see them, went one morning before we were up, and was not back at the breakfast hour. Miss Rumah, after waiting a little, ate her own breakfast, with great deliberation and composure, and then, letting the table stand, kept us waiting till he should come. The clock struck eight, nine, ten, and still he did not come. What long hours were those! for ours were the appetites of children. If she had fasted with us, we could have borne it better: as it was, we thought her cruel. We sat gaping by the fire, going often to the window to look if he were coming. He came at last, with a somewhat anxious face. Our mother and Maria were very ill, but he hoped not dangerously. He expressed surprise, and some displeasure, that we had not had our breakfast. These are specimens of Miss Rumah; I will not detail our various grievances.

This woman that disliked children so much, I must remark in passing, afterward married, and had children of her own, and spoiled them almost utterly, in her overweening fondness; whence I conclude that there *is* such a thing as natural affection, though some philosophers have affirmed the contrary.

They left the hospital at length, our mother and the girls, but not to come directly home. The house had become so infected, and their recovery was so imperfect, that it was thought necessary that they should perform a sort of quarantine, at an intermediate place, for I do not remember how many irksome days. That detention through with, we understood that they were coming—coming that day! With what delight we were prepared to welcome them!

But our poor dear mother, how altered was her appearance! With difficulty we recognized her, or believed that it was she. They brought her in with care, and placed her in an easy-chair, with pillows and cushions. She looked at us, but did not kiss us, did not call us to her, did not speak to us. She *could not* speak, could not walk, or raise her arms. Such was the sad state in which our fond, active, happy mother was restored to us. We stood and looked at her for a little, and then actually ran away, and left the room, with mingled grief and disappointment. And then the girls. Alice looked natural enough; the babe bore some marks of the disease; but Maria's face was thickly pitted. They said her comeliness was spoiled for life. And now I must give the pest-house history of this part of the family.

Owing to the highly infected state of the house, our mother and Maria took the disease by contagion, apparently, before the inoculation had time to operate. Our mother was severely, indeed, dreadfully ill, with the disease itself; but her case was aggravated by injudicious treatment: she was shockingly salivated; so that, between disease and medicine, she all but died. With Maria, also, a little past two years old, the disease went very hard; and her patience under it excited admiration. Patience characterized the child, and patience, combined with energy and spirit, still characterizes the woman. Her face was so broke out and swollen, that for several days she was entirely blind. "I want to see," she would often say, with a patient, quiet voice: "it is all dark here; won't you light a candle?" Meantime, her mother was aware of her situation, heard her voice, and her inquiries after her, but could not bestow the least attention on her. The poor thing complained that "the bees were stinging her." The doctor gave her over. It was thought she would not live till another morning. A sailor and another man sat up to watch with her. She asked for water —begged for water. "Mother! where's mother? Man, won't you give me some water?" The doctor had forbidden cold water, but to the sailor's heart her pleadings were irresistible. "I tell you what," said he to the other, "the doctor has given her over,—says he shall do no more for her

—says she cannot live. And now, I say, let us give the little thing as much cold water as she wants, and if she dies, we will not tell of it, and if she lives, we've done no harm." They did so, and she soon drank a quart. She became quiet, slept, and was wet with perspiration. In the morning early the doctor was at the door. "That child is dead, I presume," said he, inquiringly. "Dead!" replied the sailor, "she's worth a dozen dead children." She is still living, and, as you know, sustains an important position in society, as a minister's wife. Nor was her face spoiled, as used to be apprehended. For a number of years she bore marks of the disorder very visibly, but gradually and finally outgrew them, in a good degree. It is a face I love to look at, for the sincerity, the kindness, the health, and energy, and heart, of which it is the index.

A painful consequence, to her and to us, of our mother's helpless state, was, that she could not, in the least, resume her care of us. She was an observer of what passed in the house, but could direct nothing, correct nothing. In all except the sympathy and care of which she was the object, she felt herself to be, and was, in fact, a cipher.

Meantime Miss Rumah, *Aunt* Rumah, as we children satirically called her, remained with us as superintendent of domestic affairs; and if any thing could spoil the tempers of children, it was such a temper as hers acting constantly on theirs. Many vexations and petty wrongs we suffered, which our mother witnessed, but could not remedy. Miss Rumah appeared not in the least to appreciate her maternal feelings, or to think herself accountable to one who was not in a condition to interfere with her management, either personally, or by speaking to her husband; for a voice once musical and pleasant could not now utter a single articulate sound, even so much as *yes* or *no*. Nor to our mother herself were her attentions any more considerate and kindly than to us. If, for example, her broth was brought to her too hot, and she turned her lips from it, to signify the fact, "Take it away," said Miss Rumah, "she is not hungry." She could eat no solid food, and her mouth was extremely sensitive to the temperature of drinks. Why did my father retain such a woman? I do not know. Perhaps he could not find a better. And he did not know the worst at the time; for commonly ill-natured people have two tones and faces, the one all gentleness and smiles, the other crusty and forbidding. In his presence she was not what she was in ours. However, I would not do injustice to Miss Rumah. She might be better than she seemed, and mean better than she acted. She was naturally peevish, and lived herself under the thickest of the cloud she cast over others. We did but share with her, with lighter hearts than hers, the continual dropping of a very rainy day.

What occasioned our mother the most uneasiness during this long season of suspension was, that we were receiving no religious instruction. Indeed, we were exposed to influences of a contrary tendency, in the thoughtless and worldly conversation of those about us. Our father, though correct and moral, as I have said, was not pious. There were no pious persons in or about the house. If we went to bed at night, or rose in the morning, without repeating our prayers, there was no one to remind us of the omission. I do not think we did altogether neglect that duty. For myself, I can remember, that I used to repeat, with, I imagine few omissions, especially at night, either the Lord's Prayer, or that other little prayer which a child, once taught, never forgets, "Now I lay me down to sleep," etc. How much of prayer, adapted to a child's comprehension, do those four simple lines comprise!—a sense of God's care, dependence on him, the uncertainty of life, and a soul to be saved or lost. And yet I have seen the use of it, and, indeed, of all prayers *said* by children, objected to by writers on religious education, as liable to beget a habit of formality. There may be danger on that hand, and so there may be in the use of any prayer, however various or extempore. A fixed, stereotype form may lead to it more rapidly. But the greater danger is, a habit of not praying at all. That habit we were left liable to form.

Our mother began gradually to recover the use of her limbs, and at length was nearly as active and efficient as before. Her voice also she recovered in a considerable degree, but never perfectly. She had been an excellent singer: that gift was gone—gone wholly, to be restored only in heaven. This was a painful privation to her: for melody, of heart and voice, had been one of the sweetest of her enjoyments—a delightful part of her devotions; a pleasure in her cheerful hours; a recreation in her weary ones; a relief if she was sad.

And the loss of it was a loss to her maternal influence. The cradle loves the mother's lullaby, and the older child feels its mind instructed, and its heart impressed, by the music and the moral of a mother's song. She sung to us no more.

She resumed the care of her family, and Miss Rumah went away, to our—perhaps to her—relief. But she had lost ground with us, in respect to our moral training, which, I have often heard her say, it cost her much pains to regain; which she never did regain fully, in the case of any of us, there is reason to believe, but especially in the case of the youngest, whose minds were unformed and tender in proportion as they were infantile. And this is to be remembered among the hindrances she suffered in rearing her family. Children are like plants in a conservatory, which must be kept thriving. The injury they suffer from even a short neglect is generally permanent. By renewed assiduous care they may be brought-to partially, perhaps in a good degree; but they will hardly be as vigorous and blooming as they would have been. Let any Christian mother—yourself, for instance—suppose the experiment to be made in her own case. Let her suspend, entirely, her care of her young children, and hand them over to others, persons not religious, however decent or moral, for two susceptible years, and then receive them again, having passed from the respective ages of ten to twelve, eight to ten, six to eight, and so on down to the infant in arms, that comes back to her two years old, all grown strangers now to her maternal sympathies and instructions; and she will imagine what loss her children will have suffered, and how much her labor to train them up for happiness and heaven will have been increased.

CHAPTER V.

The great Ends of Domestic Education.—Physical Education.—Mental Culture.—Littlepark Castle.—An Opposing Influence.

As our children increase in years, we realize more and more the difficulty of satisfactorily conducting their education. For their spiritual well-being, especially, our concern grows deeper. While they are little, we have but to pray for them, and give them such simple instruction as they are capable of receiving; and in case they die, we can confide them to Him who said, "Suffer little children to come unto me, and forbid them not, for of such is the kingdom of God." But, as they grow older, we feel that their accountability becomes greater, and their temptations more numerous and powerful. Their peculiarities of temper, bias, habit, are more developed, and require a stronger and more skilful hand to direct or to restrain them. We find ourselves surrounded with young observers and thinkers, having senses, appetites, and passions, with an illusive and infectious world opening before them like a fascinating drama. And we find our work grown and growing, upon our hearts and hands, to a magnitude of responsibility and difficulty that we had not understood in the lisping, prattling age of the subjects of our charge.

So it was with our parents, yours and mine: their solicitude for us grew with our growth; and we can never duly appreciate our obligations to them, except as we appreciate the ends which they sought to secure, both in us and for us, and review the difficulties through which those ends were to be reached.

To speak particularly of the obstacles my mother had to contend with, would be wearisome. Some of them were of an ordinary kind; others were peculiar. I shall allude to them, more or less distinctly, as they fall in my way.

The objects of her desire and aim for her family were the following: First, their sanctification; secondly, their intellectual improvement; thirdly, their physical well-being; and fourthly, their temporal prosperity, or worldly thrift. These several ends comprised her scheme of education, and received her attention, respectively, according to their importance. What parent, in his senses, would strike out any one of them as superfluous? And yet, how many are there who omit the first; or, if they include it, place it at the bottom of the scale! But, indeed, they cannot admit it and place it there, for to admit it at all is to confess its paramount importance. How many reverse the entire order of the list,—sacrificing health to gain, fashionable accomplishments, or other forms of worldly good; regarding the cultivation of the mind, especially in a high degree, as comparatively undesirable, and treating the interests of the soul as last and least of all!

As to our physical education, she had no difficulty. Neither luxury nor effeminacy had any advocate in the house; and if she herself had been inclined to favor weakling habits in us, which was far enough from the fact, our energetic grandfather would have shamed us out of them. Indeed, I think our training in this particular was carried a little too far in the right direction; for some of us have, in later years, impaired our constitutions by our too great indifference to exposure and fatigue.

Respecting our mental culture, her views were

just and elevated. She fully appreciated the intrinsic and enduring value of knowledge; and as the pecuniary means were not wanting, she most earnestly desired that we should enjoy the best advantages that could be had. It was fortunate for us that our minister, Mr. M——, kept a school, a kind of domestic academy, in his own house, in winter, where, along with his own children, he taught a number of the youth of his parish, and a few from abroad. This school was an admirable one in its way. The good man not only taught us the common English branches, and Latin and Greek, if we chose, but he opened to our perception various wider fields of knowledge, into which we peeped, as through a half-open gate, but could not, for the present, enter. This he did to let us know that there were "more things in heaven and earth" than arithmetic and grammar, and so to make us thirst after higher acquisitions, to be prosecuted after we had done with school studies. He was also always giving us, incidentally or directly, valuable hints and counsels respecting manners, morals, and whatever concerns the intercourse and interests of human life, as well as much judicious instruction of a more religious kind. His manner was his own: he taught us in a simple, unpedagogical way—in a kind of *peripatetic* way; for he walked up and down the long "study," conversing with us here and there, and sometimes took us abroad, to instruct or exercise us in the open air. I have not often seen a private school, or a public one, comparable, on the whole, to that. The house was romantically situated—and that was something to us, for scenery has much to do with mind—and had various little works of rustic taste about it, constructed by him and his amiable family. As a school—not as his *residence*—he gave it the name of Littlepark Castle; for he knew the power of names. He was a man of true dignity and politeness, and had seen much of the world, having been an officer of the Revolution. How many happy, and, I trust, improving hours, do I remember at Littlepark Castle!

But we could not be received there till at a certain age. Until then, we were sent to the district school. I should not now remember, I presume, the first time I went to the district school, in my neat, close-buttoned jacket and trousers, but for the surprise I felt at being praised by the teacher for knowing every letter of the alphabet. I thought it no such great attainment, for I had gone beyond that, my mother having taught me, as every mother or elder sister should, from A to Z, at least. Such a character as an a-b-c-darian ought never to be seen at the district school, to drag out a winter, or a summer, in the tedious process of acquiring that incipient learning *there*.

Considerable as the advantages afforded by the minister's school were, for so retired a parish, they did by no means meet, to their full extent, our mother's wishes. She desired to add to them, both for her sons and daughters, the benefits of a residence, longer or shorter, away from home; where they might not only receive instruction in matters of learning, but have the benefit of some acquaintance with the world. In new circumstances, new impulses are imparted to the mind; in other families, if correct and refined, home habits are confirmed, if they are good, and corrected, if they are bad; and polish is the effect of mutual attrition. False ideas of society, want of naturalness when he enters it, a sort of refined rusticity, at best, are the effect of always keeping a young person within the sound of his own parish bell. For W. and me she wished a collegiate education; but *that* was beyond what she thought it expedient to propose. However, she communicated the wish to her minister, and he sounded the "powers that were;" but there was no favorable response. He said to her, "Do not be discouraged. All this property is at God's disposal; he will turn it to some good account; who knows but he will educate your sons with it."

In these views my father accorded with her, generally, and she was straitened in him only as he was straitened in his father. He had not the firmness, if he had the power, to carry out her suggestions fully, in opposition to his wishes. My grandfather was desirous, certainly, that his grandchildren should have a respectable *common* education; especially his grandsons. So much was necessary to qualify them for business. But, as the chief end of man was to get money, why expend money beyond what was necessary to that end? If a collegiate education was mentioned, he deemed it sufficient to reply, that men of learning seldom get rich. And so, of whatever profession, or pursuit in life, we might incline to follow, the standing test was, Is it the way to wealth?

Was my grandfather miserly, or sordid? He was not esteemed such. He was but an instance, of which there are thousands in the world, of a man of uncommon natural powers applying those powers inordinately to a good and lawful, but inferior end. He loved us, he sought our welfare; but sought it only in that direction in which he thought it alone, or mainly lay. It was but natural that what he chiefly valued for himself, he should chiefly value for his descendants. And it should be remembered that he received his earliest ideas on this subject in a country where wealth, next to rank, was the basis of respectability, and was, indeed, essential to the respectability of rank itself.

My grandfather stood opposed, therefore, to the educational views of our mother, as to the extent of them; and, I may add, to those of her children: for from her, or from within, they had received similar impressions of the superior value of the endowments of the mind. I remember a somewhat amusing testimony to this, in the remark of a worthy, but uncultivated old lady, whose religion, or whose preachers, rather, taught her to fear human learning, as an enemy to grace: "They are a likely family of children," said she; "but it is a desp'ate pity they are so taken to larnin." A *more* desperate pity it is, to have a desire to learn, and not the means. There is no young person for whom I feel a truer sympathy than for him, or her, who sighs for knowledge and refinement, but whose circumstances utterly forbid the desire to be gratified.

However, my mother's views prevailed in part. By one means or another it was brought about that most of us enjoyed some seasons of instruction at seminaries abroad. But it cost her some censures from the upper house, and sometimes added to her domestic burdens. She did the best she could for us, and more than most women in her circumstances would have done. What we lacked in seminary privileges, she endeavored to supply by helping us to books, and encouraging us to read at home.

It hardly occurs to me as necessary to say, that she was not actuated by ambition; it was not that her children might *shine*, that she wished them cultivated, but that they might be qualified for usefulness and happiness.

CHAPTER VI.

Religious Culture.—Temporal Prosperity.—Character of Men and Maids.—
Michael Bruin.—Spirit-drinking.

An appeal is often made to the gratitude of children in view of the pains their parents have been at for their *physical* and *temporal* welfare. " Think how tenderly they nursed you in your infancy—how many sleepless hours they suffered on your account—how anxious if you were sick—how they toiled and denied themselves to feed and clothe you through so many years of childhood and dependence, to provide for your tuition, and to lay up property for your future benefit." An appeal of this kind is certainly just; but it is not in *these* things that the strength of the appeal lies, to the children of *pious* parents. No; it was our *spiritual* welfare that cost them most; it was our moral character, rather than our outward circumstances—our eternal interests, rather than our temporal, that gave them most concern. Hence their unwearied and protracted pains with us in the way of instruction and warning; their distress for us, if we sinned; their tears shed in secret; their unceasing prayers; and their hope deferred while they looked for our conversion to Christ.

It is with reference to the obligations of my mother's children in this particular that I am now to speak. And in doing so, I can find no better method than that already adopted, of looking at the matter in the light of its circumstances.

And first, her many cares. Besides her nine children, there was always a number—often a large number—of work-people, men and maids, the domestic oversight and care of whom devolved on her. I have seldom seen a mother the amount and constancy of whose household duties exceeded hers. These cares made it impossible for her to devote as much attention either to the mental or the moral improvement of her children as she would.

Great temporal prosperity is another circumstance to be mentioned as affecting our religious training. The longer I live, the more I am impressed with the difficulty of rearing a family safely and happily in the midst of worldly wealth. The medium condition—neither poverty nor riches

—is the safe one : safe for the young as well as for the old, and for families as well as for individuals. Ours was not that medium condition. We were familiar from our birth with abundance and increase. Our mother was aware of the dangers resulting from this state of things, and endeavored to avert them. This she did, by impressing us with the vanity of riches, their instability, and their proper uses. We were favored, also, with uninterrupted health. To sickness and bereavement we were for many years strangers. Happy exemption, if it touch the heart with gratitude, but dangerous if it beget, as it too often does, security and presumption. All know that they are mortal, and are warned by a thousand providences not to boast themselves of to-morrow; but how differently is the admonition regarded, when languor and paleness in the house, anxieties and watchings, actual death, subduing grief, and weeds of mourning, enforce it on the heart! Our mother endeavored to turn all our prosperity from a source of danger to a means of spiritual good, by impressing us with a sense of our many and great obligations to our heavenly Benefactor. If this were always done—if parents would cherish, both in themselves and in their children, a grateful sense of their obligations to the Author of their blessings, worldly prosperity would less often prove a calamity than it does.

The business of a large farm required a considerable number of work-people, especially in summer; the character of these modified, to some extent unfavorably, the moral atmosphere with which our young life was invested. They were seldom pious; nor were they often immoral. They comprised, at different times, a large variety of characters—humorists, men of sense, rustics, sophists. I remember, with special dislike, among them, a great misanthrope, a great hector, and a great churl; and I also remember individuals of strong native sense, excellent temper, and considerable reading. The laborers on our New England farms, collectively taken, are, as you know, not men whose minds are wholly blank. They are Yankees, and not hinds and peasants. As they worked together in groups, or were taking their dinner, as they often did, under a shade in the field, and when they came in at night, they would be engaged in conversation. They would tell anecdotes and news; discuss opinions, characters, and politics. Not unfrequently the topics treated of in the pulpit on a recent Sunday would come under their review, and occasion such discussion as their respective talents, prejudices, or modes of faith prompted. Their talk was often entertaining, sometimes instructive; but too often it might be characterized as evil communications that corrupt good manners; foolish talking and jesting, which are not convenient; a multitude of words in which there wanteth not sin; instruction that causeth to err. It was unavoidable that we boys should more or less be listeners to these conversations, and be more or less endangered by what was evil in them. Their general effect on our sentiments and manners could not but be apprehended with some uneasiness by a Christian parent.

However, this sort of intercourse had its better, as well as its worse effects. It early acquainted us with common men, and common things; a sharp debate would stimulate our intellects; a witty repartee, or a facetious story, would occasion innocent and wholesome laughter; satire, well bestowed, made us despise the subjects of it; and the hardy, cheerful industry of men that ate their bread in the sweat of their brow, was a wholesome example as opposed to indolence and luxury. And these men, moreover, with all their diversities of mind and manners, were but a part and parcel of that human world in which we had, and were to have, our being, and with which we must, sooner or later, unavoidably mingle. It was safer to commence acquaintance with it then, under the watchful eye of parents, than at a later and unsheltered age.

The character of the maids corresponded, generally, with that of the men. Perhaps it was inferior. They were not always what they should have been. It was difficult to find such then, as now. In some cases it was necessary to dismiss them for their censurable morals.

The men were mostly comers and goers with the seasons; but one was so permanently with us that he grew to be, in his own feeling and in ours, almost as one of ourselves. Fourteen years he lived with us uninterruptedly, and more or less afterward; and he is so blended with all my early recollections, that I must beg leave to make you a little acquainted with him. Nor is the mention of him irrelevant to my subject. For no object, not even an inanimate one, much less a human being, with which our childhood was familiar, and which has infixed itself in our feelings and memory, can have been wholly neutral among the influences that have contributed to the formation of our character. The image of Michael Bruin is as early, distinct, and imperishable with me, as any my memory retains. He was with us from our infancy, and his partiality for us made him believe there was not another set of children equal to us in the world; and I presume he is of the same opinion still, if living; which I may say without incurring the charge of vanity, as I am not his endorser in the matter, and do but quote the opinion of Michael Bruin. All his affections centred in us. He had no other domestic attachments. His eye followed us in our play; his ears were always open to our voices. He was fond of startling us with his presence where we least expected it. If we strolled into the fields and woods, all at once there would be Bruin, standing before us in our path, or casting his stealthy shadow on us from behind. We thought him endowed with a kind of ubiquity. He shook down nuts and apples for us from the trees. He came in great storms to fetch us home from school. Many of his ways amused us. One of his habits was, to deposit his money under any flat stone he met with about the farm; and there it would remain, perhaps, for weeks, or till he had occasion to use it. We called such places Bruin's pocket-books. Whether it was from his fondness for us, or from his conceit of wisdom, I cannot say, but he appeared to think it incumbent on him to have some share in our discipline. This he would do, by giving us harmless counsels touching our childish heedlessness, our childish fears, and the like; but more frequently by *tutoring* us, as he called it, that is, scolding. With his tenor voice, and head aslant, and peculiar phraseology, he would berate us, for the half hour together, about no matter what, so he had some pretext for his humor. And if he raised our temper, it pleased him all the better. His figure was tall, straight, and thin, and his physiognomy peculiar, but not disagreeable, or dull. He had no idea of mental improvement, and though he could read, he seldom did. He knew, without the least vanity, whatever he thought it desirable to know, and for the rest, was ignorant without embarrassment. Indeed he seemed not to be conscious of any lack of information, for he would readily enter into conversation with any one that chose, on any subject. Nor could you ever attempt to inform him on any matter, or give him any news, but he would answer you, "I know it." Or, if your news surprised him, he would say, "Well done!" These were his customary phrases; and we children, observing his use of them, used to fabricate or feign matters for the sake of hearing them. Had we told him that Bermuda had floated to Cape Cod, he would have said, "I know it;" or if we had surprised him with the news that the man in the moon had come down, he would have said, "Well done!" Though correct in his morals, he appeared to be wholly unimpressible in regard to religion, owing perhaps to some unhappy peculiarities in his parents. Being spoken to on that subject, "I know it," said he; "religion comes natural to some people; it never came natural to me." Alas! his is but the case of the "natural" man every where. My mother desired to be useful to him, in respect to his spiritual interests, and I hope her endeavors in that way were not wholly lost.

Bruin was certainly a very original character, and in one respect a genius: for he would relate

stories impromptu beyond any person I ever knew
—pure fabrications, of great length, often, comprising a deal of incident, and very entertaining, but altogether improbable. They were generally, but not always, harmless in their effect upon a young imagination. We had a perception of his amusing eccentricities, and were not insensible to his fondness for us, though we disliked his *tutorings*. At length he married one of the maids, and went to live in a house which had fallen to him by inheritance. It was situated, quite alone, in the midst of a little picturesque wild, some two miles from us, whither we made many a pleasant excursion, going and returning through fields and woods. On these occasions both he and his wife would receive us with unfeigned pleasure. They would fill our hands and pockets with nuts and apples, fennel, bark of slippery elm, etc., and would make a sumptuous entertainment for us if they could induce us to stay for it.

No one whose memory does not extend beyond the commencement of the temperance reformation, can have any idea of the quantity of liquor that used to be consumed. Every body drank it, every where, in every house; in every business, on every pretext and occasion. And the public mind slept over the most tremendous evil that ever invaded the world since the fall, idolatry and the man of sin excepted.

For myself, I was as familiar, in my boyhood, with decanters as with teacups. Sideboards and pantries were filled with them. In every outfit in the morning for the fields a jug of rum was as regularly included as were implements of labor. Who could work without rum? There was no end to drawing cider. There was no end to making and distilling it.

We, I think, were as temperate a community, and ours as temperate a farm, as most others; but I tremble to think of the habits of that time. Our placid river was distressed with vessels bringing rum from the West Indies. It was not necessary that they should take their cargoes to the city to find a market for them: the demand was every where, and they rolled out their scores of hogsheads on the wharfless meadows—on the very grass we mowed.

This picture of the spirit-drinking past will help us to conceive of the anxiety which considerate parents then felt for their sons and daughters. They were surrounded with consuming fires. Let us thank God, my friend, that *our* children were not born to see that day, and that from such anxiety we are in so great a degree delivered.

With regard to us, I attribute it, first to God, and, under him, to a watchful and praying mother, that we were not all made drunkards. The temptation met us at every turn, and in every form, and she warned us unceasingly—warned us of the incipient habit, the growing appetite, and the awful sequel, adding and assuring us from Holy Writ, that drunkards shall not inherit the kingdom of God. Such was the impression she made on me, that I said, none hearing me but God, Let me die now, rather than ever become a drunkard. Why should not any youth say so, with the drunkard's cup, the drunkard's self, and the drunkard's end before him?

CHAPTER VII.

Conflicting Views and Agencies.—A Mischief-maker.—Importance of a Father's Aid in the Religious Training of Children.

I have mentioned the repugnancy between my grandfather's views and my mother's in regard to our intellectual education. In regard to our *religious* education, I am not aware that he ever opposed her directly. He had too much conscience to do that. And I doubt not also that he had some latent feeling for our welfare in that particular. In what human bosom dwells natural affection without some measure of such feeling? He knew that religion was a solemn matter. I have reason to believe that his convictions on that subject were deeper than his outer life manifested. Still, he was ever impressing us with those worldly sentiments which are antagonistic to godliness. If any man love the world, the love of the Father is not in him. His influence, in the nature of it, was, to say the least, as a neutralizing leaven. It was more than that; it *must* have been; for neutrality of influence, or of will, where Christ is concerned, is impossible : " He that is not with me is against me, and he that gathereth not with me scattereth abroad." Indeed, the line upon line, and precept upon precept, of his counsels, and the whole force of his character and example, went to make us worldly, and not pious. He knew that the wisdom by which my mother sought to be directed was not the wisdom that governed him, and that its tendencies were to other issues than those which he preferred. It was natural that that perception should awaken feeling, and that that feeling should express itself in action.

No parent could more faithfully inculcate than she did, the duties of industry and frugality. She gave to property its just value. Regarded as a gift of God, we were to be thankful for it ; regarded as a talent intrusted to us, we were to improve it to his glory. But whether regarded as a talent or a gift, she wished us to feel that it was inferior to intelligence and virtue. So the Scriptures represent it: " Wisdom is a defence, and money is a defence ; but the excellence of knowledge is, that wisdom giveth life to them that have it." And, by the way, did you ever notice a beau tiful marginal reading to this passage ? The Hebrew word rendered *defence*, signifies a *shadow*, that is, a protecting shade. Here are two sheltering shades. Both are grateful. But one is superior to the other, as the soul is superior to the body. The one protects us from such evils as are incident to poverty; the other protects us from the miseries of the mind: it refreshes and restores the soul. Our mother, I say, would by no means have us contemn riches. But she deprecated that supreme regard for them to which the entire atmosphere about us, and our grandfather's influence in particular, would naturally lead us. In many respects his influence was good. His strong character, and large experience in the world, qualified him for a wholesome action on boys especially: it was impossible that sloth and feebleness should feel any self-respect in his presence. But in the particular now in view, she thought it incumbent on her to employ a countervailing influence. This she did without ever opposing his wisdom openly and directly, or seeming to have any reference to it. She simply impressed us with her own independent views. And on this, as on all other subjects, she made the Word of God speak for her: "Riches are not the chief good Wisdom is the principal thing; therefore get wisdom; and with all thy getting, get understanding. Riches are not satisfying. The eye that loveth silver shall not be satisfied with silver; nor he that loveth abundance with increase. Riches are unstable. For riches certainly make to themselves wings; they fly away as an eagle toward heaven. Riches, without the grace of God, are corrupting. The love of money is the root of all evil; and covetousness is idolatry. Riches are but of brief possession. For we brought nothing into this world, and it is certain we can carry nothing out. Riches are not forever." She appealed also to experience. "I have never seen," she said, "that riches, of themselves, make people happy, or essentially and permanently respectable." And she gave us the history of some of the largest properties she had known. In one case a growing and insatiable avarice had been the rust and canker of the soul, bereaving it of good, both in a temporal and in a moral sense. In another, heirs had quarreled. In others, children had been corrupted —had destroyed the peace of parents—had squandered, to their own ruin and disgrace, the property which years of toil and self-denial had accumulated.

It is a delicate thing to draw, in the child's mind, the just line as to the value of worldly wealth. It has a positive and a relative value; and the danger is, that he will either over-estimate or under-estimate the positive. In our case, between two earnest influences, it was hardly possible that we should not do one or the other, and I think the under-estimate prevailed with us rather decidedly, for not one of us has made wealth—I may almost say a competency—an object of pursuit.

In fine, between the daughter-in-law and the father-in-law, there were two unsympathizing agencies, touching the education of her children, both intellectual and moral, running through the entire period of their youth, coincident in minor matters, but diverse in the greater. It was a protracted *race* of influences. "Two worlds at strife." Each of the parties was conscious of its existence; but neither of them avowed it, or ever made distinct allusion to it. On his side were great energy of intellect and will, great knowledge of human nature, patriarchal supremacy, habitual and admitted sway, and the power to enlarge or abridge our earthly possessions at his pleasure. On her part were a mother's love, a mother's watchfulness, a mother's prayers, and God's authoritative word. On her part were "covenants of promise" which God never forgets, a faith which he never disappoints, and a striving Spirit which he withholds not where those covenants are pleaded. More were they that were with her than they that were with him.

He was irritated that he could not neutralize her power; sometimes even to resentment. There were times when, for weeks, he would not enter the house. He would only ride to the door, and request to see my father on business. These unhappy moods his daughter-in-law seemed not to notice or perceive. If he refused to dismount and come in, she had a pleasant salutation for him from the door, or a cheerful greeting at the gate. As he was fond of a long pipe, she kept a supply of them expressly for him, and would sometimes send him out one ready lighted to puff upon his horse. These kind attentions were always shown in a manner so sincere, cheerful, and unembarrassed, that he could not find it in his heart long to resist her gentleness and goodness. How great is the power of meekness! And how marvelous it is that this power-loving world is so slow to perceive that power and practice it!

I have mentioned my grandparents' housekeeper, Deborah. She was the evil angel of the house, as it regarded us. She was a single woman, selfish and envious, but a good domestic manager. She had just religion enough, such as it was, to be very self-complacently and thoroughly bigoted, being of that sort of people whose faith the Scriptures describe as being without works, and therefore dead; without charity, and therefore good for nothing. There was no meeting of her order in the place, and so she seldom worshipped any where. If it was suggested to her that she might perhaps receive *some* benefit from meeting with the people of the place—that possibly she might get *some* edification through the prayers and sermons of our good Mr. M., her answer was, Why seek the living among the dead? But I have no concern with her religion, nor with herself, except as her influence affected us.

How often does a weak mind originate or direct in particular cases, the action of a strong one through a knowledge of its weak or sensitive points—as a weak hand can put a match to combustible materials, or a feeble breath blow a sleeping fire! Deborah had never read Locke, yet she understood, practically, the fact of the association of ideas, and made frequent use of it to set things a-going in a mischievous direction in my grandfather's mind. Had she offered him her advice directly, on any subject, he would not have paid the least attention to it; but alas! who suspects approaches, made in the guise of friendship, on his blind side? or waits to ask what finger touches the chafed and sensitive spot before he winces? She made his prejudices her study, and well knew how to disturb them. If he was inclined to be dissatisfied with any thing proposed or done in his son's family—if he was distrustful or impatient of a power in his daughter-in-law obstructive of his own, it needed but an allusion, a surmise, a suggestive word, to put such discontent in action. Often, when his feelings, left to themselves, would have flowed on placidly and smoothly, she would find some stone to cast into the bed of the stream, to ruffle and make it turbid. Her influence was a hidden one, but palpable in its effects. It was aimed chiefly at my mother, who was well aware of it. She knew the source of many a distorted view of herself and of her concerns, and of many an irritable feeling and unpleasant mood in her father-in-law. But she had too much self-respect to notice it. She kept the even tenor of her way, wrapping herself in her conscious integrity, and letting the clouds pass without being chilled by them.

I have mentioned that my father had a sister. She was the father's favorite in their childhood. That partiality continued, and was extended to her children. They lived at a distance, beyond his sight and supervision, and did as they listed; and I know that some of their ways and notions were such as would have drawn on *us* his severe displeasure. They came, now and then, in dresses somewhat finer than we wore, to visit him and our grandmother, bringing, usually, besides the pleasure of their company (in which we shared), some luxury to gratify them. We, of course, had no objection to this, nor they any objectionable motive; but we could hardly help remarking that a fat turkey from the L——'s went farther with our grandparents than a thousand personal services done for them by our parents and ourselves, the year through. This was a reflection of our own, and not our parents' suggestion.

Now Deborah was wont to make much of the L——'s; not that she really cared for them, but it was her policy. To flatter them, was to gratify my grandfather; and to flatter them, was not necessarily to disparage us. But Deborah knew how to make the one involve the other. One of the commonest and meanest arts of sycophancy is, to put one object in the shade by merely placing another between it and the light. We loved our aunt. She was a generous-minded woman, and Debby was no favorite with her. And we loved our cousins; they were pleasant children. But we could not be quite insensible to the injustice done us through them. However, if any real injury resulted from it, it was to our cousins, rather than to us. Better for any child to be the subject of neglect than of favoritism.

In fine, this sister of "the coppersmith" did us much evil. The *suggestive* Debby. I love openness, even in the wicked. I hate your indirect, *suggestive* mischief-maker—one that abuses our better feelings through our worse ones—one who relates to us an anecdote, or talks with us on some common-place topic, and leaves our respect or our charity for some neighbor abated, we cannot tell whence or why—one whose very pity, or whose very praise, blasts, we know not how, the character of a brother. If it were worth while to find a motive for her, other than in the invidiousness of her nature, it was, by ingratiating herself with the man she served, to secure for herself a home in his house while he lived, and a legacy at his death. These ends she realized.

I must here do my grandfather the justice to say that, in the end, he came to think better of my mother's aims and methods—not, however, till near the conclusion of his life. He had, indeed, always respected her, and loved her children; but he seemed to manifest greater confidence and greater complacency in them now, and predicted well of them in future. One of his last acts was, to add a verbal codicil to his will—it was too late to do it formally in writing—giving to each of his grandchildren a sum of money: "And let them spend it, if they will," said he, "in getting an education." In the twilight of two worlds—on the dusky verge of the valley of the shadow of death— how is the moral vision enlightened and enlarged, often, to take in a wider, and a clearer, and a juster view of things!

What added most of all to the embarrassments my mother suffered from the sources I have mentioned, was the fact that my father was not pious. Could she have had his sympathy and aid, she would have felt herself greatly sustained. "Two are better than one," whether to withstand a pressure from without, or to carry a common burden. But alas! there was here but one to resist the pressure, and to bear up the burden. There "was one alone, and there was not a second." And not only so, but he that should have put his shoulder to the work, with the strength of a man, was himself a weight upon her hands, an obstacle in her path. In all other respects he was one of the best of husbands, one of the best of fathers. But as to religion, it was easy to see—*we* saw—that he had no sympathy with her. He did not *oppose*, but neither did he aid her, in her religious endeavors. Or if he did actively aid or second her in some particulars externally belonging to religion, such as commending and setting an example of good morals, attending public worship, and contributing to its pecuniary support (which last he did more liberally than any man in the parish), his real, and discernible, and sometimes out-spoken dissent from the *spirit* of religion, made his influence to be more than equiponderant in the other scale. If no man's influence can be neuter, any where, least of all can it in his own house.

> " Example strikes
> All human hearts; a bad example more;
> More still a *father's*."

I do not mean to say that his example was a bad one, in the common acceptation of that term; still, it was the example of a father not religious. The absence of religion is irreligion; and how can irreligion exert a religious influence, or fail to exert an irreligious one? If, in all a parent's plans and conversation, religion has no place—if the will of God is never referred to—if the name of Jesus is never spoken—if eternity is never mentioned, or practically regarded—if there is no religious instruction, no family prayer—what is the natural effect of this upon the child? And then it is easy to conceive a thousand specific cases, or a general course of conduct, where the child, finding the father's sentiments or practice more agreeable to his natural inclinations than the mother's, decides to follow him; and regarding his authority or judgment in the matter as equal, or paramount to hers, wants no better sanction.

It was a matter of painful regret to my mother that her children must grow up without family prayer. Family devotions are a great aid to family instruction and government; nor is that their only, or their highest use. "All our instructions, like our other efforts, are in vain without the blessing of God. This blessing, to be obtained, must be asked. Prayer for the success of our instructions should accompany them of course. The child should be a witness of the parent's application to God for him, and should be taught to supplicate for himself. All the duties of religion are eminently solemn and venerable in the eyes of children; but none will so strongly prove the sincerity of the parent; none so powerfully awaken the reverence of the child; none so happily recommend the instruction which he receives, as family devotions, peculiarly those in which petitions for the children occupy a distinguished place. At the same time, God will actually bless those who seek his blessing. But where it is not sought, it will not be given ; and where it is not given, our best exertions will be in vain. *Except the Lord build the house, they labor in vain that build it."**

To bring up a family in the nurture and admonition of the Lord, is, under the most favorable circumstances, a great work; and in *some* circumstances it rises to sublimity. What are the elements of greatness, and who are the truly great ? I do not ask who the *distinguished* are ; for greatness and fame are not always coupled in this world's calendar. But if greatness be predicable of those who have attempted and achieved great things—if far-reaching views, if benevolence, patience, faith, toil, perseverance, be attributes of greatness, I know not where it is to be found, if not in the Christian parent training up a family at once for earth and heaven—for virtue, usefulness, and honor here, and glory there ; nor a finer instance of heroism than that of one parent, especially a mother, laboring for that end *alone*,— unsustained, perhaps opposed and counteracted, by those who ought to aid her, and especially by

* Dwight.

one of whom every sentiment of affection, both conjugal and parental, and every dictate of religion, both revealed and natural, demand that his aims, sympathies, and influence, should be one with hers.

CHAPTER VIII.

Marriage of a Sister.—Fire.—Sickness.—Conversions.—Incident.—Prediction.—At College.—Installation.—Conversion of a Sister.

We come now to a period when the eldest of my mother's children are fast passing out of the season of childhood and youth, and when some of them are about to be removed from her immediate influence. She had been early and diligent in sowing the seed of divine truth in their minds; she had prayed for a quickening influence upon it, had watered it with her tears, and had looked to see it germinate; but as yet it seemed to lie hidden in the soil. They were none of them, it is true, corrupted by vice; they showed a sincere respect to religion; two or three of them had, when quite young, manifested much religious tenderness: still she had no satisfactory evidence that any of them were regenerate. Yet her confidence in a covenant-keeping and prayer-hearing God was unshaken. She often expressed and stayed her faith by quoting those lines of Watts:

> "Though seed lie buried long in dust,
> It shan't deceive their hope;
> The precious grain can ne'er be lost,
> For grace insures the crop."

remember, when we were quite young, as we were all taking our breakfast together, by ourselves, in our chatty way, an old gentleman came in, and sat looking at us thoughtfully for some time. Turning to our mother, he said, "You have more happiness in your children now than you will have hereafter; for by and by they will be broken up, and all scattered here and there, and you will be saying with Job, 'Oh, that it were with me as in days past, when my children were about me!'" He might have added mentally, "and some of them will die," for such had been his own experience as a parent. I looked up and listened. That was a new idea to me, or, at least, I had not reflected on it—that we were going, by and by, to be separated from each other, and from our fond parents, and our happy home, and all scattered here and there. It was a thought not wholly pleasant to me.

But now, at the date at which we have arrived, that remark of the aged man began to have its fulfillment, in the marriage of our eldest sister. This was of course a very interesting event to us, but when she actually came to leave us, we were surprised at the suddenness and painfulness of our regrets. We had looked forward to a ceremony, with a pleasant party and entertainment, and had overlooked the parting that was to follow. Susan had been a very affectionate and helpful daughter, and a fond sister. To me, especially, her love and care had been almost matronal. But I did not think it became my manliness to shed tears at parting with her, as most of the household did. So I stood apart, leaning on the fence, combatting my feelings, and keeping my resolution, as my eyes followed her, going down the road that led to the place of her embarkation for her new and distant home—going, with a heart at once sad and happy, from one Eden to another: I stood thus, keeping my manful resolution, when my little sister Rebekah, climbing up at my side, and turning her sympathizing face up into mine, "John," said she, plaintively, "is not Susan going to live at home *any more?*" That question was too much.

A few months pass, and in the middle of a

FIRE—SICKNESS. 93

summer night we are awakened by a cry of fire. My brother and I sprang out of bed, and ran to see it. We needed no time to rub our eyes open; a fire was a rare sight there: we had never seen a fire. It proved to be an anchor factory, a mile from us. In one of the buildings there were several thousand bushels of coal, all ignited, which made the heat intense. I looked on only (as all might as well have done, for there was no arresting it), while my brother went to work at once, with great zeal, among the thickest of the men. They continued their efforts till sunrise, and then looked like so many sons of Ham, being perfectly black with smoke and coal-dust, and streaming with perspiration. In this heated and exhausted state, a number of them, and my brother among them, plunged into the pond to wash. The pond was remarkable for the coldness of the water. We returned home, and went to public worship, for it was Sunday; and my brother appeared to feel no inconvenience from his imprudence. The day following, however, he suddenly fainted, and fell on the floor. He was dangerously ill.

And now our mother was affected with a twofold anxiety. She was anxious for his life, and still more for his soul. She prayed for him incessantly and fervently. For many days his recovery was doubtful; but at length he reached the crisis of his fever, and began to mend. And *then* his heart melted. We heard him singing on his bed, one bright and lovely morning, as he lay alone: it was a new song put into his mouth, even praise to our God. That sick-bed had been blessed to him, and I shall never forget the emotion which she manifested who had watched over him with so deep solicitude. To her it was as life from the dead. So, in one respect, it was to us all. To her it was an answer to her prayers, a blessing on her endeavors, a first-fruits of her maternal faith, an earnest of the future. It added another praying soul in a house where hitherto hers had been the only one,—if faith be requisite to prayer.

The change in him was a striking one, and the time now permits it to be said, a permanent and saving one; for by their fruits shall ye know them. Heretofore his mind and drift had been altogether worldly; now the great question with him was, how he could be most useful as a servant of Christ. He determined on an education and the ministry;

to which our father made no objection; but our grandfather opposed it decidedly. This grandson bore his name; he was the most like him of any of his grandchildren; and on him he seemed to have fixed his hopes as the one most likely to add to the estate, and bear up the name, which he was about to leave. He tried every means to withdraw him from his purpose, seconding his arguments with the offer of a valuable property. But his mind was fixed: he entered at once upon the requisite studies, acquired a thorough education, classical and theological, and entered the ministry.

How often does God follow up religious instruction and make it effectual by means of afflictive providences! It was so in the instance of conversion which has been mentioned. And so it was in the next that occurred in our family. Our married sister suffered a very tender bereavement in the death of her first-born, a lovely little daughter of eleven months. I remember the conclusion of her letter apprising us of the event: " I will no more think of her as *dead*, but as a lamb in the bosom of Him who has taken her to himself. It is there that we must find her, if we would hope to see her again. 'I shall go to her, but she will not return to me.' Dear mother, pray .hat this affliction may be sanctified to us." It was sanctified.

My own conversion to Christ followed, as I humbly hope, not long after. I was leaving home to be absent three or four months. I had said good-by to the family. My mother followed me to the door, and said a few words to me respecting my salvation. I could not but perceive that she felt very deeply concerned for me; for I was very thoughtless at the time, though not always and habitually so, and was going among thoughtless people; and to relieve her mind, I said to her, "Mother, you need not be so anxious about me. I know that religion is important; I have always intended to be a Christian, and I shall be, before I die." "Ah! that," she replied, "is what disquiets me. You *intend* to be a Christian, and on that you rely. You are looking for a convenient season, which will never come." That interview left some solemnity on my mind for a time, but it was soon dissipated among the strangers whither I went. However, a few weeks after, it pleased God to call up my attention to the subject in a manner too impressive to leave me either able or disposed to throw it off. From that hour, and once for all, I trust, till I reach eternity, my mind was sleeplessly awakened to the realities concerned in the soul's salvation. This it pleased God to do directly, as from himself, without any one conversing with me, or other apparent means. Why I was then and thus awakened I cannot tell; I attribute it to a mother's prayers.

I will not detail the various states and emotions through which I passed from darkness to light; but I will mention an incident which occurs to me here, connected with one of my first attempts to do good as a Christian.

There was an evening meeting. It was rather numerously attended, in that particular instance, especially by the young. It was conducted by a venerable man, a deacon of the church; who, having made an address, turned to me, and said, "Here is my young friend, Mr. ———, present, who hopes he has given himself to Christ; I presume he will be willing to address us." I had never attempted to speak in public, but I knew not how to decline. I could not resist the look of expectation which all eyes were turning upon me, seeming to say to me, as Cornelius to Peter, "Now therefore we are all here present before God, to

hear all things that are commanded thee of God."
My recent seriousness was known, and was one
cause of so many coming together. I rose trembling, therefore, and spoke with a tremulous voice;
addressing the young only, and I well remember
in what drift. I took the "convenient season"
which I knew *they* were allowing themselves to
trust to, as *I* had done, and in few and kind words,
showed its delusiveness, its presumption, its ingratitude, and its folly—just as my own thought
and conscience had analyzed the matter in my
own case. I have reason to believe that my
conversion, and that address, were made a means
of impressing many. A revival of religion followed. But the particular incident which I proposed to mention, was the following: Some ten
years after, passing through a remote corner
of that parish, or the one next to it, I entered a
solitary house to inquire my way. The woman
greeted me with a smile, and then with tears, and
begged me to sit down. "You do not know me,"
said she; "but I know you. Do you remember
making an address to the young people at ——
church, at such a time?" I did remember it.
"Well," continued she, "my daughter died three

weeks ago, rejoicing, and praising God for that address, which was the means of her conversion." How much good we do, or may do, we can never know in this world. That seed was scattered farther than my humble thought anticipated when I made my feeble exhortation. My dear friend, let us sow beside all waters. And *in the morning* sow thy seed, mind; and then, of all the good thy children do, thyself will be the grandmother, yea, and the ancestor of all the good which thy children's children, and the whole line of thy posterity shall do, down to the world's end.

> The good begun by thee shall onward flow,
> In many a branching stream, and wider grow.

I had before had a strong desire to be educated at college, but not with a view to the Christian ministry. On the contrary, the fear that, being educated, I might perhaps be led into that profession, had held me back. My mother had often expressed her belief that I should one day be a preacher of the gospel, and my own conscience suggested to me that, in case I were educated and converted, my duty would lead me to be one; and so, like a prudent man foreseeing the evil, and hiding himself, I thought it safe to forego the education. But now, if the Lord enabled me, and counted me faithful, I desired no other work.

I had sometimes pleasantly replied to my mother's prediction, that, as I had no desire to be a minister, not the least, nor any prospect of going to college, there was little likelihood of its being fulfilled. "Perhaps so," she would say; "but we shall see." It certainly was, as circumstances were, including the Scotch king's influence, a very improbable thing. I have since asked her why she entertained such a belief, and so confidently. She said that she had dedicated me from my birth to that work, if the Lord should see fit to call me to it, and had done it with such prayers and such desires as, it had seemed to her, he would not disappoint.

To an education and the ministry, therefore, my mind was now most ardently directed. And how happy we were, my brother and I, to find ourselves within the walls of the same college, though in different classes. I think that brothers have rarely loved each other better than we had done; and that early and fond attachment and companionship was enhanced now, by sameness and sacredness of pursuits. Religion and study had partially separated us for a time: religion and study now united us more closely than ever. Would it have been so with us, had we been borne and nurtured by an unbelieving mother?

That question reminds me of a scene that furnishes its answer. I was at the installation of that brother over a numerous and interesting flock. A large portion of them were present at his examination by the council. Being through with their inquiries as to his literary and theological qualifications, "There is one subject more," said the moderator, "respecting which we should like to be informed by the candidate—*his personal religious experience.*" A deep and sympathetic silence pervaded the room at this question, as if it were felt by all present that here was a matter at once the most important and the most delicate of all. The candidate, after a moment's pause, said, "I had a pious mother." What a rush of feeling, what a tide of recollections, did these words bring to my heart and memory! And I believe, from their effect on the audience generally, that those words alone, in the manner in which they were spoken, though he had added nothing to them would have satisfied them that they might confide in the genuineness of the piety of him who was about to become their spiritual guide. Indeed, was not the fact of a pious mother a kind of pledge, even in an apostle's view, of the piety of the son, especially when the *mother's* mother was also pious? "When I call to remembrance," says Paul to Timothy, "the unfeigned faith that is in thee, which dwelt first in thy grandmother Lois and thy mother Eunice, and I am persuaded that in thee also."

I do not propose to speak of each particular case of conversion in the family. The next after my own, with an interval of three or four years, was that of Maria, of which I will say a word. She was a girl of a good deal of spirit naturally; she loved the world, and long resisted her religious convictions. Being on a visit to sister Susan's, S. offered her a new dress if she would read Doddridge's Rise and Progress through. She accepted the proposal; and if mere energy of will would have carried any one through, it would have been likely to do so in her case; for she did nothing with half a mind. But the book disturbed her conscience so, or was otherwise so unpalatable, that before she had half finished it, she flung it down in great vexation, exclaiming, "I *will not* buy your dress so dear!" The conviction of having often resisted and grieved the Spirit at length came upon her with such force that she fell into despair, and for a time her case was painfully interesting. Flesh and color wasted rapidly under the power of her feelings. However, the grace of God prevailed to her deliverance. She was enabled to give herself to Christ; which she did in the bloom of her youth, in the midst of prosperity, and when the world looked brightest to her.

CHAPTER IX.

My Father.—His Moral Character.—Constitutional Peculiarities.—Sympathetic Emotions.—Death of my Grandfather.

I have thus far said little about my father. He was a man of the most native kindness I ever knew. Indeed, I have never known a near approximation to him, in this respect. He could not bear to disquiet or disoblige any living thing. I think he would have delayed the felling of a tree, if possible, certainly with considerable inconvenience to himself, to accommodate a bird that had built her nest in it, till she should be through with rearing her young. If the cat got his chair, he would let her keep it, and help himself to another. I have known him turn out of his path to avoid disturbing a flock of geese that had gone to sleep in it for the night. Animals perceived his kindness, and confided in it. The cattle would follow him when he crossed the pastures, and his voice would call an animal from a thicket or hidden dell when another's search for it had been in vain. Old Richard, the family horse, though a spirited animal and an excellent parade horse, felt at liberty to go to sleep when he mounted him, fearing no uncomfortable urging from his all-tolerant master. Sometimes the spontaneous attentions of his brute acquaintance would be rather ludicrously embarrassing to him : he came home one morning from a walk to a neighbor's, a mile distant, accompanied by nine dogs. "I am ashamed," said he ; " but the creatures came out and attached themselves to me, one after another, as I passed their homes, refusing to be sent back ; and so I have gone and come with all this retinue."

We were so accustomed to these exhibitions of his kindness, and its effects, that we scarcely noticed them ; but visitors were much amused with them.

If the brutes perceived these dispositions in him, it may be supposed that men perceived them also, and that they often took advantage of them. Of that I shall speak hereafter; for the present I must speak of his character in its moral and spiritual aspects.

His moral character, externally and negatively regarded, was irreproachable. No man could charge him with any vice or injustice. He felt and manifested respect for religion; was a regular attendant on public worship; contributed freely for the pecuniary support of the gospel at home, and among the heathen. No man was more considerate of the poor. He was an affectionate husband, a fond parent, a most obliging neighbor.

"Enough," some will say. "You have decribed a good man—a character that Heaven cannot but approve and accept." But without *faith* it is impossible to please God. And though I bestow all my goods to feed the poor, and have not *charity*, it profiteth me nothing. He had not faith—did not profess to have; nor that charity which the apostle makes essential to a holy character. Christ was not precious to him. He was not a praying man, in his family, nor probably in secret. He did not "love the brethren," as such, and as they love one another; though he respected and confided in them as good people. He had no delight in religious conversation. His heart felt, and sometimes manifested, aversion, as every unrenewed heart does, to some of the essential truths of the gospel—to *the* truth which, comprehensively taken, *is* the gospel—that of a gratuitous salvation through faith in Christ, rather than by works.

In fine, whatever else he was, he was not a Christian. And, indeed, the very qualities which were so estimable in him appeared to operate as a bar to his becoming one. There is probably something constitutionally peculiar in every individual which becomes a peculiar obstacle to his coming to Christ. In his case, it seemed as if a temper so equable and placid, so osier-like to external influences, bending to the zephyr, and not broken by the tempest, was hardly susceptible of those deep convictions, and those earnest strivings, which they experience who enter in at the strait gate. When a man has strong passions, rough points, palpable sins, there is that in him on which religion may fasten its convictions. He knows, and does not deny, that he is a sinner. The currents of his soul are like a strong ebb meeting with a powerful wind: the conflict throws it into commotion. But when the character is all made up of gentle dispositions and amiable morals, religion acts upon it as the zephyr upon the tranquil lake, rippling its surface, but not agitating its depths.

He often experienced a kind of sympathetic effect from religion, as many do. I have, for instance, seen his eyes fill at the sight of a Sunday-school procession. But it was a superficial, momentary feeling—a sympathy without convictions or purposes—a deceitful species of religion of which there is a great deal in the world, very transient, and very worthless. Jerusalem was full of it while Jesus was riding into that city in the midst of hosannas. Romanists are full of it in connection with their splendid pageantries. Constantly to renew and flatter such deceptive emotions is one of the arts of the Romish Church.

It was to be feared also, that he leaned on his morality as affording some ground of confidence as to his acceptableness to God. He *knew* better; and so does many another who rests on such a basis notwithstanding. We are all pharisaically inclined—alive without the law—till the Spirit makes us otherwise.

He was, moreover, full of earthly blessings. He had never known want, or the fear of want; had never experienced sickness, or any afflictive bereavement; in a word, had never known adversity of any sort, up to the fiftieth year of his life. And they that know no earthly want are not apt to be sensible of spiritual want.

He had passed the age I have mentioned when his father died, leaving one half his large property to him, and the other to his daughter

The "Scotch king" was gone! with all his energy and thrift, with all his supervision over his own affairs and ours. And not only we, but the numerous laboring men that had been wont to depend on him for employment; the business men that had looked to him for loans; the whole surrounding region that for half a century had been conscious of his presence and his movements, seemed to come to a pause, and to be at a loss to accommodate themselves to the vacancy that had occurred. When such a man dies, it is felt to be no ordinary event. Apart from the moral lessons which it teaches, almost every man within the range of his acquaintance feels that it touches some interest of his own. There were little minds that felt their envy relieved, to see the tallest tree of the wood removed; but there were others, and perhaps those envious ones themselves, that soon missed his sheltering shade. The mainspring was broken that had kept their wheels in motion.

His last days demand a passing notice. I was

with him the last few weeks; he would not suffer me to leave him, night nor day. He was aware of his approaching end. His eyes were opened to the realities of the unseen world. Withdrawing them from this, he found them filled at once with that, as the traveler who, at sunset, turning his back to the glowing west, sees the night gathering and approaching from the dusky east. There are but two worlds, two interests, that we are concerned with, and while the one engrosses us, the other is forgotten. He had long been occupied with this; he now felt that he had done with it. He surveyed his life, with deep deliberation, from childhood onward, comprising eighty-one years, and expressed the result, with agonized emotion, in these words: "*God has given me a large share of this world; I fear it is my only portion!*" There are those to whom those words of Jesus come home at length with dreadful pertinency and meaning: "Wo unto you that are rich! for ye have received your consolation; wo unto you that are full! for ye shall hunger." The valley of the shadow of death! how dismaying to him that comes upon it unawares and unprepared! Once, in his youth, while descending some dangerous rapids (those of Lachine, I think), in command of one of a flotilla of batteaux going to attack Montreal, a number of them being lost, and his own in imminent peril, he seized an oar, and by his skill, vigor, and presence of mind, carried her through, thus saving himself and his company from destruction. But here was a passage before him that he felt himself unequal to; it needed a stronger arm than his; and he felt that he had no right to expect that arm would now appear for him.

I was often awaked in the night by his distress, less of body than of mind. And then, though I was young in religion, and in years, and he had not been wont to confer with striplings, he would request me to rise, that we might talk of the concerns of the soul, and supplicate the divine compassion in his behalf. He gave me, in those midnight hours, his religious history, which, from his early youth, alas! was all a blank. At sixteen, he told me, he experienced for a short time great light and comfort in his mind. "Why did those happy, hopeful feelings leave me? But they were all dissipated by our removal to this country, and the scenes that followed." In connection with these reminiscences of his youth came remembrances of his mother, the venerated Agnes. And I now saw, in what he felt and expressed, how faithful she had been—that pious mother—long, long ago, as it seemed to my youthful inexperience of the rapidity of time, when this now aged and remorseful, if not repentant man, was a docile listening child, and knelt at her side in prayer. Oh! why do we forget the prayers, and tears, and pious counsels of believing parents? Why do we wander thus from "the instruction of our father," and forsake thus "the law of our mother?" "For they shall be an ornament of grace to thy head," says Solomon, "and chains about thy neck."

But God does not forget. He remembers, and brings to our remembrance, those early prayers and counsels often at the eleventh hour, to the saving of the soul. I trust it was so in this instance. And it is in this view of it chiefly that I introduce this piece of history; I look upon it as a striking instance of the faithfulness of a covenant-keeping and prayer-remembering God, and of the undying power of a mother's early influence with her child. Here were fountains that had been choked up with the rubbish of this world

DEATH OF MY GRANDFATHER. 113

for fourscore years, till their existence was forgotten and unknown, now reappearing and gushing forth anew.

He continued in much the same state of mind for several weeks, but at length expressed a humble, diffident hope of mercy, and it was pleasant to converse with him. The day before he died, a dark cloud passed over him, and he was filled with great distress. It seemed to be the hour of Satan's power with him. But the tempter and the cloud departed, and light and peace returned. At evening he lay so still with inward thought that we apprehended his end was near. He had through the afternoon been unable to speak. But bending over him, I breathed an inquiry at his ear respecting his mental state, when, to our surprise, he answered, in a distinct and strong voice, "*Full of peace and joy in the Holy Ghost.*' He requested to be raised up, took some refreshment, and said, "If it please God, I am willing that this should be my last supper." He conversed calmly and delightfully for some time, and continued in the same comfortable frame through the night. In the morning he died. His mental faculties were undecayed.

He gave to each of his grandchildren some valued thing to be kept as a special memorial of him: to me his sleeve-buttons. They were taken from the wrists that had worn them forty years, and handed to me. They are marked with his initials, and are a thousand times more valued for his sake than for the material, old British gold, of which they are made.

We regarded him with sincere affection and with much respect while he lived; we mourned his death; and he still fills, and ever will, and in most respects agreeably, a large place in our recollections of that early portion of our life.

CHAPTER X.

Pecuniary Losses and Embarrassments.—Morality of the Endorsing System.

My father felt his death in more respects than one. He missed him not only as a parent, but as one on whom he had always leaned, in business matters, with almost childish freedom from great care.

It was an event that increased, apparently, the dangers of his spiritual state. As principal executor, a large amount of labor was devolved on him in the settlement of the estate; and the property he inherited brought with it such temptations as are incident to worldly possessions. To some of these temptations, such as luxury, pride, rapacity, his habits and dispositions made him little obnoxious; but to others, such as complacency and trust in wealth, he was more open; and perhaps I should add the flatteries which worldly prosperity occasions. Wealth maketh many friends, says Solomon; but the possessor has need to distinguish between *its* friends and his.

However, when, in the providence of God, riches make to themselves wings and fly away, they take their temptations with them and leave a salutary lesson behind. The inheritance, in the present case, proved to be an inheritance of cares, vexations, disappointment, and chagrin. My father's universally obliging disposition was well understood, and there were always those who were willing to take advantage of it. He could not say *No*, to any applicant. Not that he was ignorant of human nature *generally ;* he was aware of the existence of fraudulent dispositions and practices among mankind, and of the doubtful promises of such as had pressing necessities to relieve, urgent creditors to satisfy, or visionary schemes to undertake ; and yet, in dealing with men individually and personally, his better judgment availed him nothing, because he allowed himself to believe that the man he dealt with was an exception to the rest. Indeed, if a person came to him with a plausible, or a piteous story, it did such violence to his nature to distrust or to deny him, that the pain of it was greater than the pain of possible deception or loss. My memory might furnish you with a copious history of wrongs done to his confiding disposition, in lesser matters and in larger, sometimes amusing, often exciting indignation, and altogether affording a rare, and perhaps instructive commentary on human nature.

If his kind acts had been prompted and directed by Christian principle, they would have been more judicious, and better requited—in heaven, if not on earth ; but they had not, apparently, any religious motive.

While his father lived, his influence had operated a good deal to restrain his accommodating propensity, and also to keep off applicants : but now that he was gone, and my father had both more liberty and more means, he was beset by all sorts of persons asking his assistance. If any wanted money to pay a debt, or to buy more land, or to set up or enlarge their business, they would come to him to lend or underwrite. It seemed as if every body looked to him to help him out in his wishes, schemes, and troubles. Of those thankless people commonly called *sponges*—people of niggardly cupidity, or indolent improvidence, who are always availing themselves, in small ways, of a liberal neighbor's kindness—I will say nothing.

In some instances he was a substantial benefactor, in relieving an embarrassed worthy man, and putting him upon a footing of prosperity. In others, he did but make bad worse; for there are many who will relax their efforts and stand still, or run deeper in debt, in proportion to the means or credit they can command. To lend to such is adding opium to drowsiness, and paying out rope to a sinking man. He made numerous very obliging, but very unfortunate loans; some of which were never repaid, and others came back to him in the shape of property unsaleable and valueless.

These minor losses, often repeated, might have seriously embarrassed, or made him poor, in time; but his indiscretion did not stop at these. A young merchant failed, and involved him for some four or five thousand dollars as underwriter. This, though a serious loss, was not a ruinous one. There were two men in a neighboring town, twins by birth, and brothers in deceit, who were engaged in a great western land speculation. They had large farms in western New York, whole townships in Ohio, with various other huge slices of the forests of the West. With a capital of six and a quarter cents they would not have hesitated, I presume, to contract for the whole Valley of the Mississippi. They had also a store of goods. They were men of most insinuating address, of the greatest subtlety, capable of any depth of deceit. They exhibited false lists of their property and debts, to satisfy their creditors of their solvency, ten times over. They even made a profession of religion. I do not say they did it expressly with a view to gaining moral credit, and, through that, pecuniary credit; but it served them to that end. My father himself confided in them on that ground. When we expressed our fears, and said, "Those men appear to us too plausible to be honest," he would reply : " Why, they are professors of religion—members in good standing in Mr. K——'s church." They were, in fact, generally confided in as honest men ; they were believed to be wealthy, and were largely trusted by banks and individuals. But for religion's sake, I will mention here, that opinion, as to their honesty, was fully reversed in the course of events, and that they were ejected from the church.

To induce my father to endorse for them, to a

considerable amount, they gave him a mortgage on several large tracts at the West—enough for a grand-duchy. Once on their paper, he found it difficult to withdraw from it ; and, indeed, he increased his liabilities, most imprudently, from time to time, lest, by withholding his name, he should bring on a crisis in their affairs which he at length dreaded scarcely less than they. It was a part of his imprudence that he did not fully communicate the matter to his family. We knew, indeed, that he was in the toils of those subtle men, but had no idea to what extent.

Thus things went on, waxing worse, for several years. The men kept up appearances, out-faced suspicions, deceived every body. Some of the most cautious of men, near neighbors, and best acquainted with them, were taken in by them, to their ruin. But by and by they came down with a crash, as *we* had long anticipated, and others had begun to do, bringing ruin and dismay upon many worthier than they ; taking care, just before their failure, to obtain at one of the banks a loan of six thousand dollars. They asked for ten thousand. Of that loan they never gave any account to their endorsers, except in the significant remark, that "their families must live." Nor could any body tell what became of other moneys they had borrowed.

They went West; were taken ill simultaneously, and died at the same hour—or *gave out* that they died! For as no one was allowed to see them in their sickness, or in their coffins, it was afterwards suspected that their exit out of the world was a feint to elude their endorsers, some of whom had followed them. I incline to think that their reported death was a reality, though a feigned one would not have been at all inconsistent with their character. However, they *disappeared*—going the way of all the earth, or elsewhere. The simultaneousness of their exit, if they died, was singular. Twin brothers to the last.

As for my father, the first knowledge he had of their failure was an *official* one, in the shape of attachments on his property. The agent of one bank and another hastened to secure their claims. I need not give details; there was levy upon levy, and mortgage upon mortgage. Still, he did not imagine himself to be ruined, his property being much larger than his liabilities. But the banks, by trafficking among themselves, embarrassed him still more, and, indeed, contrived to make the most of him. On some of the largest notes there were several joint-endorsers with him, who were pledged of course to share the responsibility. It was a joint responsibility that they themselves contemplated; it was a joint responsibility that the banks accepted; and it was palpable unrighteousness, bad faith, downright cruelty, to disregard that fact. Yet this the banks did. By a process, of which I will not trouble you with a description, they managed to make my father pay the whole. The object was, by freeing the property of his fellow-endorsers from those particular claims, to make it available for other claims elsewhere. Three of those soulless corporations put their heads together in this magnanimous conspiracy. It was *legal;* was it *righteous?* And was it righteous in that bank that loaned that last six thousand dollars, *knowing*, as the president confessed to me, that the men were essentially and desperately insolvent at that very moment, and that the endorsers would have it to pay? But the endorsers were good, and that was all he cared for. There were banks in very corrupt hands at that time.

GROWING EMBARRASSMENTS. 123

The banks were every way unaccommodating. They did not mind making expense; and feeling quite safe in the amplitude of their securities, they would receive nothing but the whole amount in cash, which it had become impossible to raise. Every dollar of his stocks and money had been paid over to them, and yet the mortgages remained, covering every acre, every building, every mortgageable thing. Meantime a wasting interest was consuming him.

But those western land securities—what became of them? They were but a parcel of the general calamity. In attempting to have recourse to them, we were met with expensive suits, by other and prior, but to us unknown claimants. The suits went against us, and there was good money sent after bad. That reliance was a quagmire, treacherous to the foot—a millstone hanged about the neck. Of course the men knew this.

In fine, my father found the difficulties of his situation inextricable and interminable. He was greatly straitened, if not absolutely poor, for the remainder of his days. It was a sad reverse, an over-cast sky permanently dark, and growing darker, to one who, from the morning of his days, had never known the slightest passing shadow of adversity. And he was the more chagrined because he had all along acted in opposition to the fears, wishes, and expostulations of his family.

Meantime, his family were hardly in a condition to suffer such a reverse without great and lasting inconvenience. Our parents were at a time of life when competency and increasing release from care, instead of want and effort, are essential to tranquillity and enjoyment. Nor was this all. My father had recently received a personal injury which quite disabled him for a while, and was a cause of suffering to him through life. My elder brother had but just finished his professional education, and I was in the midst of mine, from which the catastrophe called me off at once, and impaired my health and constitution, in the efforts I made to arrest and mitigate the mischief. My sisters next younger than myself were just at an age when young ladies find it particularly unpleasant to be thrown into a condition of bankruptcy, real or reputed. Then my two young brothers, and Rebekah, had yet their education to acquire, in a great degree. And finally, the profession which we elder brothers had in view was not of

CALAMITIES PROTRACTED. 125

that lucrative kind that would enable us to do much, in a pecuniary way, for the rest.

But there was a *providence* in it—an irresistible and wise providence—having reference to results which we did not see as yet. We had done our best to arrest the mischief, but it had gone on in spite of us—like a desolating water, bursting its embankments, and assuming forms, and taking in agencies, in its progress, which it was not possible for us to foresee, or counteract.

If, like a conflagration, it had soon done its work, and ceased, it would have been less afflictive. Though it had left us but the ashes of our prosperity, it would have left us free to build again. But this was a tornado that not only prostrated the house, but encumbered us with the ruins; from which we could not extricate ourselves. They lay upon us, and we could not stir, or breathe. In its train came years of fruitless efforts, costs, consuming interest, suspense, failures, disappointments. Our better way had been, to abandon all at once, and go to live and prosper elsewhere as we might. For myself, I would not again go through with the waste of time, of feeling, and of health I suffered, in my protracted effort to disencumber and redeem, not for myself, the homestead portion of the property, for any money. But it was our HOME, and I could not bear to think of my parents and sisters being forced to quit it.

The first human pair bade adieu to the sweetest abode that earth ever knew; and in the gloomiest circumstances: and I imagine that *one* of their heavy thoughts, as they cast their eyes behind them, was, that it was their *home* they were leaving—the place of the infancy of their being and their early joys. Indeed, so Milton represents it, in Eve's lament. True, " the world was all before them, where to choose;" but in all that world's width there was not another *home*, nor would have been though there had been another Eden. In that one feature of their exile how many of their children have been like them! There is but one spot on earth that we can ever truly call our home. We may have many residences, and local attachments; but those peculiar and most cherished associations which pertain to the place of our birth and childhood cannot be transferred or reproduced elsewhere. That spot we always quit with regret, whether to leave it desolate, or to see it occupied by strangers.

Our home was pleasant. Every thing about it—every rock and tree, every spring and streamlet, every prospect—was associated with our being, and blended with our feelings. We had built a new house, ample and convenient; we had embellished it with trees, shrubs, flowers, and graperies. But—I may as well say here—it all *went*—finally. It was like a land-slip on the coast, that, with "ruin steep," sinks suddenly at first to a lower level, and there rests, apparently, inviting you to rebuild upon it your half-demolished house; but it still keeps settling, slowly and deceitfully, till it is all submerged, at length, and not a tree, roof, or chimney-top remains visible.

But it is a satisfaction to say, that we kept a tolerable footing on it while our father lived. Then we could quit it with less feeling.

For myself, I most seriously question the *morality* of the endorsing system. There are Scripture warnings against it; Prov. xi. 15, and vi. 1–5. Why? For *moral* reasons, doubtless; and not merely prudential ones in a worldly respect. And if it were from prudential reasons only, I have no right to ask my neighbor to do what prudence forbids his doing, and from which the Bible dissuades him. I believe the system to be iniquitous in principle, and corrupting in its tendencies. Look at it. If a moneyed institution, or an individual, lends money, he does it for a valuable consideration, namely, the interest. Let the lender, then, take the risk, along with the compensation; and not throw it upon a third party, who has no share in the profits of the transaction, nor any power to direct its management. One of two things: the borrower is either responsible and honest, or the contrary. If the one, his signature is sufficient for the lender; if the other, let the lender see to it. It is his concern, and not some other man's. Make the supposition that there is an express or implicit *understanding* between the lender and the borrower, as there often *is*, that the latter is irresponsible, and that the endorser will have to pay the debt: no one will question the palpable unrighteousness of this. It is nothing else than a conspiracy to defraud. Is there not, then, unrighteousness in every case in proportion to the degree of reliance placed, by both or either of the parties, on the endorser? A *partial* and understood reliance upon the surety is of the same moral nature as an *entire* and understood reliance.

MORALITY OF ENDORSING. 129

The difference is only in degree. In the one case the third party is a *probable* victim; in the other, a *certain* one.

And then, the system, by affording undue facilities for credit, encourages all sorts of injudicious business undertakings and adventurous speculations; which it does to the demoralizing of society. The system, moreover, tempts the cupidity of banks and capitalists. Many a loan is made with the known moral certainty, or is so managed by extensions of credit, or renewals, that it *becomes* a certainty, that he that is surety "shall smart for it." I have given an instance of this in the six thousand dollar loan, when the bank knew beforehand, both the fact of the borrower's insolvency and the endorser's ignorance of that fact. And yet the president enforced the payment of that sum with as little mercy or compunction as if he had missed it from his vault, and overtaken it with hue and cry, in the hands of the man of false keys and dark lantern.

I do not say these things as a *burnt child*. And I know what arguments are used on the other side. With me they weigh little. Nor do I forget that I am writing to a lady, who may not feel much interest in these bank matters. But you have sons who may, through you, when they are older, derive some wisdom at least from the subject.

CHAPTER XI.

The Day of Adversity.—A Concert of Prayer.—Conversion of our Father.—His subsequent Life and Death.—Agnes Buchanan.—Descent of Character in Families.

In adversity consider. This was a day of adversity with us: it behooved us to acknowledge the hand of God in it, and to derive that spiritual benefit which he no doubt intended. It became the religious members of the family especially, to pray and endeavor that it might be turned to the spiritual good of us all. On the unconverted and younger members the calamity fell heaviest. They did indeed "consider;" but alas! as we all are too apt to do, they considered the calamity itself rather than its uses. They would contrast our former condition and prospects with the present; they would reflect on all the knaveries that had been concerned in producing the change; on the ingratitude of the men whom their father had been so ready to oblige; on all the aspects of the matter, and would break out at times, the girls especially, with expressions of the deepest vexation, each in her characteristic way. All that was natural. Do not judge them harshly: do not call it feebleness of character, thus uselessly to vex themselves. If you have never experienced a similar reverse—never known what it was to have been affluent yesterday and poor to-day, and to feel the change for your parents', and your sisters' and young brothers' sakes; and to reflect, too, that all this came from abused confidence and kindness—you have no just conception of the aggravations of the case.

But that reverse was showing them how much they had been setting their affection on things on the earth, and how unstable was the ground on which they had been fain to build the edifice of their bliss.

Our mother felt the change very sensibly ; but more on her husband's and children's account than on her own. However, she endeavored to take a cheerful and Christian view of it, and to lead her family to do the same. "Our property is gone," she would say; "but the best things are left to us—our lives, our health, our character How much worse to have suffered the loss of these! And besides, the fountain of all good is still open to us—the favor of God. Seek first the kingdom of God and his righteousness, and all these things—these lost things, so far as you may need them—shall be added to you. Trust in the Lord, and do good; so shalt thou dwell in the land, and verily thou shalt be fed. If to health and youth you add diligence and prayer, you may still hope to be prosperous and happy. To be cloudy and disheartened is unamiable and unchristian. Fret not thyself because of evil doers, neither be thou envious against the workers of iniquity. And, most of all, let us beware of murmuring against God. What! shall we receive good at the hand of the Lord, and shall we not receive evil? Let us be sensible of all the good we have received, and are receiving, at his hand; and let us believe that all things work together for good to them that love him."

How invaluable is prudent Christian counsel in such circumstances! When I see—what so often happens—a young family plunged into adversity by the sudden failure of the father, I am desirous of saying to them, "The best things are left to you—life, health, and character; add to these diligence and prayer, and you need not fear." There is a beautiful device which I have seen—a group of lilies, in a time of drought, their heads drooping almost to the ground, with the motto, We shall rise again. I need not make the application.

As it regarded my father, the effect of the reverse on him was this: it had dissolved the charm of worldly prosperity. If it had not weaned him from the world, it had dimmed its brightness. It had not soured his temper: he was the same man of kindness still, in feeling and in act. Though by no means insensible to the wrongs he had suffered, he forbore to express himself with virulence and wrath against the authors of them. It had changed his relations with selfish and worldly men. No longer able to confer favors on them, he was no longer beset by them. That was a happy riddance. It had had an effect to humble, but not to break his spirit. And, fond though he always was of his family, it had seemed to increase his regard for them, and his love for their society. In all this there was ground to hope that his troubles might be blessed to him.

But the loss of his property was not all he suffered. God had taken other methods with him in the way of chastisement. I have alluded to a personal injury. A little before the two failures, that of the young merchant, and that of the twins, he was seized with a sudden illness which for some days threatened to be fatal. He had hardly recovered from that, when he fell and broke one of his limbs, besides being generally shocked and hurt by the fall. The fracture was a bad one, and the limb was badly set, and worse re-set, by unskilful surgeons. For months he lay on his bed in much anguish, and when he left it he was lame for life. This appeared to affect him more, on his own account, than his losses. Those touched his substance; this, his person. He had hitherto been an erect and active man.

Thus was he visited with a complication of troubles. But no means, whether providences or truths, or both combined, are effectual to the renewing of the mind, without the converting grace of God.

He had reached the age of sixty-five. Most of his children had, as we hoped, become pious. He was still without hope, and without God in the world. The morning and meridian of his days were gone; the shadows of the evening were around him. He had experienced prosperity and adversity, health and sickness. He had lived through interesting revivals. And now his years, his habits, his characteristic propensity to put far off an evil day, made us fear, in the weakness of our faith, that his regeneration was scarcely to be hoped for. The *moral* man out of the church may be settled on his lees as well as the hypocrite in it.

But God's thoughts are not our thoughts. No one is to be despaired of so long as he yet lives, and is within the reach of prayer.

From the commencement of their union, his conversion to Christ had been the subject of the unceasing solicitude and prayer of his believing wife; and her prayer now was, that his troubles might be turned to his salvation. Discreet in all things, she was discreet in regard to his existing circumstances. When adversity came, she bore it meekly, and strengthened him—uttering no reproaches or complainings; though, had he listened to her judicious and earnest advice, he would have avoided the ruin. She had foreseen, and done what she could to avert it; but now that it had come, she met it with Christian magnanimity, judging that adversity itself is sufficient, without those aggravations of it which come in the shape of despondency, murmuring, and loss of temper—only praying, and suggesting to him, that the loss of an earthly portion might be the means of his securing a heavenly one.

But no such effect was visible. Indeed, latterly, there was reason to apprehend a contrary tendency. As his pecuniary troubles increased from year to year, they wore upon his spirit; his cheerfulness abated; he was more silent, and he seemed to be getting morally, as well as socially, more apathetic.

We, his children, had a desponding sense of his spiritual condition. Almost Christian as he had been all his days, and not far from the kingdom of heaven, it was painful to think that, to human view, he was not likely ever to be nearer to it than he was. Our mother's faith was stronger. She remembered the unjust judge, and to what end that parable was spoken—" that men ought always to pray, and not to faint." It was uttered expressly for our encouragement in an extreme case, like this. When means have been exhausted, when opportunity is almost gone, when faith is yielding, and hope expiring, then should we bethink ourselves of the importunate widow, and derive unwonted confidence from the very extremity of the case.

And if two of you shall *agree* on earth as touching any thing that they shall ask, it shall be done for them. This she also called to mind, and proposed to her children, at home and abroad, to meet with her at the throne of grace, in his behalf, at a certain hour of the day. We did so; but I am ashamed to say with how little faith on my part Touching the *thing* to be prayed for, I have no doubt we were agreed; and to that *agreement*, rather than to the degree of our faith, is the promise made. Yet there must be *some* faith, or there is no sincerity. Some faith I trust I had, and that the others had more. But, oh slow of heart to believe! How express is the promise; how unequivocally worded! Why do we not oftener, and with a more simple and unqualified faith, avail ourselves of it?

Whatever may have been the mental state of him who was the object of our concert, there was a growing intensity of feeling in our mother. Her spirit had no rest. After they had retired, one night, she said a few words expressive of her con-

A NIGHT OF INTERCESSION. 139

cern for him; he gave her an indifferent answer, and fell asleep. She arose, in the fullness of an anxious heart, and returning to the sitting-room, raked open a bed of coals, and spent the night in prayer. It was cold, being in the latter part of February. Behold the difference between the believer and the unbeliever: the one sleeps over his own impending ruin; the other wakes and wrestles for him in agonizing prayer. As the day dawned, she fell into a train of reflections like the following: " I have borne this burden forty years; I can carry it no farther; it is too heavy for me; I must roll it off on God. I feel that I have done! *I* cannot change his heart. I *can't* convert him, however much I distress myself. Perhaps I have sinned in distressing myself as I have. God may have seen in me the want of a simple reliance on him; or the want of true and absolute submission to his will. He may have seen me unwilling or afraid to commit the matter of my husband's salvation *entirely* to him. But I feel that I *must* and *do* thus commit it to him now. I will afflict myself no more. I shall still pray for him, and use such means as may seem advisable, but—saved or lost!—I leave the result with God."

No, my mother, you could not change his heart.

> The transformation of apostate man
> From fool to wise, from earthly to divine,
> Is work for Him that made him.

She was conscious of a simplicity of trust now, and a relief of mind, such as, on that subject, she had never felt before. So prayed, and found relief, the wife of Elkanah.*

In the morning, after breakfast, finding him alone, she said a few words to him, to this effect. She remarked that they had lived together above forty years; that their union had been an affectionate and happy one, and it was painful to think that they were soon to be separated without any prospect of ever being reunited; for, at their time of life, they could not expect to continue a great while longer in this world; and as to another, it did not appear, as matters now stood, that they would dwell together there. "As for me, I may be deceived," she said; "but I trust I am a Christian, and that, when I die, notwithstanding my imperfections, I shall receive mercy through Christ, and be admitted to heaven; but you do not *pro-*

---

* 1 Sam. i. 15–18.

fess to have an interest in Christ, or any scriptural hope of salvation. So that, if our respective cases are as we suppose them to be, we shall walk together but a few days here, and then our roads part, and we meet no more. And now I have this one request to make—*devote this day to the concerns of the soul;* devote it to reflection and to prayer. If you cannot do it for your own sake, do it to oblige me."

Struck with her earnest manner, he said, decisively, "*I will.*" He was "not able to resist the wisdom and the spirit by which she spake."

She saw no more of him till quite night, when he came in and sat down, sad and thoughtful, by the fire. She did not know the nature of his feelings; nor was any allusion made to the interview of the morning. It was evident that he was not happy. He had an eye more expressive of sorrow than any eye I ever saw. It glistened, but did not flow with tears, and its color seemed to deepen. Sorrow was in him a sealed fountain: it found no vent in words.

The next day he again disappeared, and was gone till evening. His countenance and manner, when he returned, were still thoughtful, but there was a serenity in his look which was not there before. "I do not know," said he to my mother, "what has ailed me to-day; my feelings have been unusual, and indeed very strange." "Why? How have you felt?" she asked. "I can hardly tell you," he replied. "I have no reason to think myself a Christian, or, perhaps, that I ever shall be; but it has seemed to me, this afternoon, as if every thing was changed. Every thing appeared to speak of God. The trees, the hills, the skies—every thing seemed to praise him. And I felt that I loved every body. If there is any one that I have hated, it is Mr. G.; but I have felt to-day that I loved him like a brother."*

His heart seemed overflowing with emotions of this kind—as new and strange to him as the expression of them was to his astonished and rejoicing, but yet trembling wife.

"Every thing spoke of God! Rocks, hills, trees, every thing in nature seemed to praise him!" So had he thought and felt, that afternoon. And this is the very language that the prophet puts into the mouth of the penitent and new-born.

* Mr. G. was a certain "revivalist," the particular type of whose zeal, or whose *tactics*, had disgusted him.

ALL THINGS BECOME NEW. 143

How often has it been uttered by those who, at the time, did not remember, or perhaps were quite ignorant, that there was such language in the Bible. " Ye shall go out with joy, and be led forth with peace : the mountains and the hills shall break forth before you into singing, and all the trees of the field shall clap their hands."

And he "loved every body." This man of gentleness and kindness, this most obliging neighbor, this doer of innumerable favors to his fellowmen, now felt that he *loved* all human kind. What! had he never loved them before ? No, not as he loved them now. It was a new emotion in him ; new in kind, in intensity, and in extent. It was a *heaven-born* love, pure and universal. This is that *charity* of which the apostle speaks.

It was afterwards known that he spent the former of those two days in a retired valley on his farm, and the other in a wood. He had engaged to spend *one* day in retirement. That he might have appeared to do merely to fulfill a promise. The second day was eminently probationary, and eminently critical. It seemed as if the Spirit tested his sincerity by means of it, and would try whether he were willing to prolong his seeking voluntarily, and unmoved by human urgency. Had he stopped at the first day, the result would, in all probability, have been finally and fatally different from what it was. How many fail by stopping mid-way in their strivings and convictions! Another day, another *hour* of seeking, with the feeling that they *must* prevail, and heaven had been gained!

On the following morning the minister of the place happened to call. He knew nothing of my father's state of mind. "Mr. C.," said my father "you have conversed with many on the subject of religion, I think you have never done so with me." Mr. C. was a truly good man, and beginning to acknowledge his fault, "Oh," said my father, "no apology is due; I did not speak of it as implying any omission of duty on your part. When a man has lived as long as I have without religion, it is not surprising that Christians should pass him by, thinking it useless to press the subject upon him any further. I only made the remark by way of introducing the subject now."

They had a long conversation, and on leaving the house, the minister said to the first Christian he met, "I have great news to tell you: Mr. ——

has become a new man. I have just come from conversing with him, and have no doubt of the reality of his conversion to Christ. The change in him is surprising; he is indeed a perfect child in religion."

There is joy on earth, as well as in heaven, over a sinner that repenteth; and it was natural that news of the conversion of such an one as he should pass rapidly from one rejoicing Christian to another, throughout the place. He, meanwhile, absorbed with his own thoughts and feelings, and not professing or supposing himself, as yet, to be a regenerate man, was quite unconscious that his case thus occupied the thoughts and conversation of others. That evening there was a religious meeting. He went to it, and finding it full (for there was a more than ordinary religious interest in the place at the time), sat down on one of the lowest benches among some children. His head was gray, and his appearance somewhat venerable; and being naturally a man of great simplicity of character and manner, he was still more so now, under the influence of religious feeling. Indeed, in all except his years, he seemed as much a child as the little ones with whom he sat. The meeting through, he was astonished to find himself surrounded by all the pious present, old and young. He knew not what to make of it. He was overwhelmed with so unwonted an expression of affectionate regard. "Even young persons," said he, in the account he gave me of his religious experience, some months afterwards, not having seen him till then—" even young persons, who had never spoken to me in their lives, whom I scarcely knew, except by their resemblance to their parents, as well as older Christians with whom I was familiar, gathered about me in that way. I could not stir for them. They held me by my hands; they took hold of my clothes, even; *they* wept, and *I* wept."

You will understand this; to those who, in themselves, know nothing of Christian sympathies, it would seem a strange, perhaps a repulsive scene —an exhibition of unintelligible weakness.

After suitable delay and self-examination, he made a public profession of his faith, receiving baptism in connection with that act.

He also joined the temperance society, which was then in the earlier stages of its existence. He had not done this before, for reasons of hospitality, in part, but chiefly on account of his work-people. He took a deep interest, as long as he lived, in that reform.

The Bible had been to him a sealed book, and a too much neglected one. He used to read it sometimes on Sunday, after the public services, but only the historical portions, generally for entertainment, or as a matter of propriety and righteousness, or to gratify his wife. But now he read the doctrinal and preceptive portions, with great docility and earnestness, improving many of his leisure hours in this way, and drawing closer to the window as the daylight waned. A part of his children had ceased to live at home; with those that remained he set up family prayer. How grateful would it be, if we could look back and remember that, from our infancy, we had been accustomed to kneel together, the children with the parents, at the family altar. We have no such remembrances; but it is some satisfaction to know that domestic worship was at length instituted, and became a part of the history of the paternal mansion, before the family all left it, and ceased to call it home.

My father lived ten years to test the genuineness of his faith. I trust he walked worthy of the vocation wherewith he was called. He bore his accumulating worldly embarrassments, and his increasing bodily infirmities, with great patience and submission. His spirit was eminently childlike—I had almost said *wonderfully* childlike. No trait of his character, when I think of him, affects me like this.

He died at the age of seventy-five. His illness was sudden, and of short continuance. His pastor, who came to see him, found him weaned from the world, and looking to another; and asking him what particular request he desired might be made for him in prayer, he said, "Not that I may recover, but that I may be prepared to go."

His funeral brought together nearly the whole population of the place; and then it was apparent how much they had esteemed him. His blameless morals, his amiable dispositions, his many kind acts, his wrongs and reverses, his late conversion, and humble piety, all rose to their minds, and they were affected with the sincerest regret.

I trust he is in heaven; and if he is, the great instrument of his conversion was, no doubt, his faithful wife. But there was another and an earlier instrumentality than hers. His grandmother Agnes, who lived till he was twelve or fifteen years old, took much pains to impress his young mind with religious things; and her instructions and prayers had, undoubtedly, through God's blessing, their influence with him through all his subsequent life.

How often does the descending stream of influence owe its salubrity to the salt some pious hand cast into it at a point so high that it has ceased to be acknowledged, or known. And how inciting is the thought that "the *good* men do (and not merely the *evil*, as Mark Antony avers) lives after them;" that our influence is not restricted to the individual, or generation, on which it is immediately exerted, nor limited by the years of our little sojourn on earth. We may act on the race at large, born and unborn; but in the line of our posterity especially, we may and *must* send our influence onwards, with peculiar energy—who can tell how far? There is no fact more striking in human history than the *descent of character in families;* none more evincive of God's remembrance of his covenant with his people; none more accordant with the natural laws of influence as dependent on the framework of society; none more encouraging to the believing parent; none more solemn to the unbelieving, who is entailing with awful probability, with moral certainty, if God do not prevent it, his own irreligion upon his children's children, down to the latest generation. May you, my dear friend, be an Agnes Buchanan, or a grandmother Lois, to a widely-branching pious posterity; and of you may it be said,

> "The sweet remembrance of the just,
> Like a green root, revives and bears
> A train of blessings for their heirs,
>   When dying Nature sleeps in dust."

CHAPTER XII.

Educational Views and Methods.—The Christian Plan.

NOTWITHSTANDING our many imperfections, I trust we may, as a family, indulge the hope that we have, through grace, all chosen that good part which shall not be taken from us; and so far as *instrumentalities* have been concerned in this result, I think we all feel that that of our mother was the greatest. And now, a review of what I have written suggests, perhaps, that I have not done what you requested. You asked for a mother's *methods* with her children, and behold a miscellany of histories and comments. However, I trust you will gather something to your purpose from that miscellany; and for the rest, I will now throw together a few reminiscences and observations, under several heads, which may be more accordant with what you desire.

She began, then, in right views of the moral nature of her children. She recognized the fact of their natural sinfulness. And hence she regarded their sanctification as the great end to be aimed at in their education. This fact and this aim are the proper basis of domestic training, as they are the basis of the divine system of dealing with mankind; man's fallen nature and his recovery to holiness being the great matters with which the Bible and a disciplinary providence concern themselves.

Not to recognize this fact and aim, in the training of children, is to proceed upon a false and defective view of things, and must, of course, involve a failure. How can we expect to mould the character judiciously and happily, while we overlook that which is so generic of character and conduct—the natural heart; and how can we look for other results than earthly and ignoble ones, while we do not aim at the higher and the heavenly?

It involves a failure, not in reference to the world to come merely, but also in reference to this. The education which is best for a future world is the best for the present. For of what earthly interest are not the dispositions and habits of piety promotive: or of what earthly interest are the passions, views, and practices of irreligion not destructive?

The Christian scheme, then, is the only true and hopeful one. Recognizing the child's inherent depravity, his accountability, his immortality, the necessity of his spiritual renewal, and the means by which that end is to be attained, it aims to educate him at once for earth and heaven.

Now what *moral power* attaches to this scheme? In the first place, the end itself, which it contemplates, comprising the interests of two worlds, is elevating and inspiring. It impresses the parent and the child with its vastness and solemnity. And then, with regard to *means*, are there any means to form the character comparable to those of which a religious education avails itself? There is the word of God, with its exhaustless treasury of precepts and motives; there is the force of Christian example; the enlightened conscience of the child; the prevailing power of prayer; the teaching of the Spirit; the concurring discipline of Providence.

And how is parental duty *simplified* by this Christian plan? We have really but one thing to aim at, since the piety of our children, the salvation of the soul, comprises all inferior good. We need not distract ourselves with the various and uncertain ways and interests of this world: "one thing is needful," and that one thing is what we have to prosecute, directly, simply, and supremely.

And how do these views *sustain* parental effort, patience, and hope? From the commencement of your relations with your child, you admit the fact of the sinfulness of his nature. You are therefore not surprised, though pained, at any development of that nature which he may make. Nor does it cast down your confidence as to his eventual character. You go to a throne of grace in his behalf. You know that there is a power to meet the case, and an ear to hear.

CHAPTER XIII.

Parental Government.—Parental Instinct.

As a disciplinarian, my mother appears to me to have been eminently judicious and efficient. Her government was mild, patient, uniform, unyielding—demanding and securing prompt, implicit, cheerful obedience. With nothing short of *such* obedience, prompt, unquestioning, and cheerful, would she be satisfied. She had one strong, far-reaching *religious* reason for this: it was her conviction that the unsubdued wills of such as have never been subject to parental authority become, in many instances, a fatal obstacle to their salvation. As they have never submitted to man, they will not submit to God. This remark of hers used to be very impressive to me.

She never lost her temper with us. I have heard her say that she was naturally quick, and somewhat violent, in her resentments, but that the feeling of anger was so painful to her that she set herself to correct it; and such was the self-control she early acquired, by God's assistance, that, from the time of her professing religion, I presume no one ever saw the least appearance of anger in her, under whatever provocation. Such self-command is a great matter in the governing of children.

She did not often use the rod; it was not often necessary; but if an aggravated fault or refractoriness demanded it, she used it effectively. She did not profess to be wiser than Solomon on this point, as many do—pleading that the rod destroys the self-respect of the child, humiliates him, and breaks down his spirit. It may do so in hands tyrannical and arbitrary, in hands summary and ruthless; or it may harden the child by unnecessary frequency in the use of it, with or without— but especially without—reproof accompanying it. The rod is not the sole, nor the principal means of a wise domestic government, any more than stocks and penitentiaries are of civil government. The temper of some children may be such that it may never be necessary to use it; in many cases the judicious use of it in a single instance may be effective for life; and if our spirit and manner be such as they should be with our children, a *frequent* resort to this species of correction can hardly be necessary in the case of any. But to denounce and discard it altogether, as some do, is what neither Scripture nor experience sanctions. "The rod and reproof give wisdom—the rod *and* reproof, the former enforcing the latter—but a child left to himself bringeth his mother to shame;" from which mention of the *mother* I infer that *she*, as well as the father, is to use the rod if the case require it. Or the wise man may here be intimating to the mother, as being naturally more indulgent than the father, that if she allow her fondness to interfere with his correcting the child, she is preparing sorrow for herself. Prov. xxix. 15. See also Prov. xix. 18, so truthfully and beautifully expressive both of the wisdom and the tenderness of the parent in this business of correction. Also, Prov. xiii. 24; which lays the charge of parental unkindness in this matter at the right door.

Another feature in her government, which I must mention, was, that she accustomed us to yield obedience to her authority *as* authority, without deeming it incumbent on her to give the reasons of her requirements, or resorting to persuasion to induce acquiescence. She would, indeed, acquaint us with the proprieties and improprieties of things, whenever she thought it necessary or expedient to do so; but in a mere matter of authority she would not stand to argue with us; it was to *herself*, and not to her reasons, that we were taught to yield. We knew—we felt, that she was a reasonable woman, and did nothing from caprice or passion; we knew that she loved us; we knew that authority was vested in her as a parent; and on these grounds we submitted to her requirements with more alacrity and content than we could have done on any other.

There are those—and among them grave and distinguished men—who hold that children are to be *reasoned* into obedience and subjection. Being reasonable beings, they are to be controlled by reasons, and not by mere authority. This is plausible; but I am persuaded, from observation and reflection, and from the Bible, that it is a fallacious and disastrous doctrine. For, first, the child is not always capable of comprehending the truth and force of reasons, any more than we are capable of understanding the reasons of the providential government of our Heavenly Father over us. What sort of care and of discipline should we have from him, if he should deem it necessary, out of respect to us as rational beings, to bring down the reasons of his procedure to the satisfaction of our understandings and our *tempers?* Would our souls, freed from the humiliating consciousness of servitude to mere authority, be enlarged and liberalized? Would our reason be more enlightened, and more modest? Would our hearts be tranquilized? Should we respect and love God more, distrust him less, and dwell in greater harmony with men? And then the parent himself is often a bad reasoner. He may have a sound head and a good heart, and yet be unskillful in rhetoric and logic. There are even judges on the bench whose strong sense, or whose prompt intuitive perception of the merits of a case, will lead them to a right decision, while, were they to attempt to give, to the satisfaction of the parties, or others, the *reasons* of their judgment, they would fail. So would it be, often, with the parent. His common sense, unexplained, his instinctive judgment, would be safer than his logic. And, finally, there is such a thing as a simple, virtuous *obedience to authority,* as such:

an obedience or respect due to the *relations* of the parties concerned, independently of the reasons on which the behests of the superior party are founded. It asks no reasons beyond the simple fact that such is the will of the superior. Such obedience is itself a virtue, and carries with it the pleasing consciousness of virtue; the withholding of it God emphatically condemns; without it there can be no subordination, no society, and no *faith*. Next to obeying God, obedience to parents is the highest and most amiable exercise of this virtue. How conspicuous and lovely does it shine in Jesus himself, who was "subject to his parents."

The method of government here objected to is equivalent to the no-government doctrine advocated in our day, and is practically not much better. It reduces the parent to the mere province of advice and persuasion, making the child the ultimate judge and director of his own conduct. You propose to control him by your *reasons*. But suppose he does not choose to listen to your reasons; as probably he will not in any matter that crosses his inclinations. You may debate all day, and forever, with him; he will never have done with his rejoinders, so long as his wishes are against you; and so, unless you will leave him to himself, you will have to resort to *authority*, after all. And then you will seem to him like one who first attempts to argue down an opponent, and failing in that, resorts to force to *put* him down.

Such is the natural course and issue of this sort of wisdom. It may do with some tempers, *possibly*—which is the largest concession I will make to it; but, in the great majority of cases, it will lead to conceit and obstinacy.

The government by authority, judiciously conducted, is more natural and easy to both parent and child. The child submits to it with greater readiness and cheerfulness; it tries his temper less. That it is easier for the parent is obvious. Respect for parental authority, once established, is, like the fear of God, a universal sentiment, acting every where and always; while on your reasoning-and-persuasion plan, every particular requirement becomes a distinct case, to be sustained by its specific reasons;—an endless labor to the parent, a ceaseless vexation to the child.

It is requisite to a due subordination in families, that each member know his proper place and relative importance in the house; and it will be no detriment to the modesty and contentment of the child to be made to feel, that if he be not the most insignificant of the members, there are at least others whose claims to respect and accommodation are paramount to his. I recall a homely incident which once impressed this matter on myself. Between my trunk and bed there was hardly room for a chair which incommoded me when I opened my trunk. I removed it repeatedly; but still finding it replaced, I thrust it under the bed; and going down, asked, in great impatience, Who keeps putting that plaguy chair between the bed and my trunk? "I do," said the maid; "there is no other place for it." "Well, I have pushed it under the bed!" "It must not be put there again," said my mother, ironically, to the maid; "we must find some other place for it: it won't do to incommode *John; John* must be accommodated, whoever else is inconvenienced; the house must be arranged as he pleases." I felt ashamed, went and restored the chair to its place, reflecting once for all, that there were others besides John whose convenience was to be regarded, and that domestic order, and the comfort of all, are to be promoted by each member, though at some sacrifice of individual convenience.

While I am on this subject of domestic government, I must say a word on the *parental instinct* in regard to it. That many children are spoiled by their parents, some by over-strictness, and more by indulgence, is not to be questioned. But with all the weakness of parents, I believe that the children are better in their hands, as a general thing, than they would be in the hands of others. There are people who, having no children themselves, are always wondering at the defects of parental management. They aver that *they* could discipline children to perfection. But for myself, I would rather trust a father's judgment, and a mother's instinct, than the combined wisdom of them all. They think that the *fondness* of parents disqualifies them for their office. But that fondness—in other words, parental love—is the very thing that fits them for it. It may degenerate into weakness, it often does; but if it did not exist, and with great force and constancy, the nature and interests of the child would be too delicate a trust to be committed to them. I speak as to parents in general. There are many whose mere humanity and piety might, in the absence of the parental instinct, be sufficient to secure a good degree of fidelity and tenderness on their part; but consider the gentleness and patience children need, and the ungentle and ungodly character of innumerable parents, in Christian and in heathen lands, and imagine in how many houses impatience, violence, and neglect would take the place of patience, gentleness, and care.

In connection with parental love there exists another feeling, equally important, though alas, in too many instances, not equally operative—a sense of parental *responsibility*. That feeling cannot exist in another bosom.

If facts be resorted to, I think that among the spoiled children one meets with, a much more than due proportion, both of the feeble and the disorderly, will be found among those who have been brought up by unmarried relatives, male or female.

The Author of the domestic institution has made parental duty as untransferable as the parental relation. He designs that *we*, and not others, shall educate our children; and he has peculiarly fitted us for it, by making our love the basis of our procedure. It is our love that makes us patient and kind, and it is that that makes us *faithful*. Love does not shun the pain of restraining or chastising them; on the contrary, it puts us upon the duty. He that spareth his rod hateth his son: but he that loveth him chasteneth him betimes. It may, as I have said, and too often does, become a weakness, and interfere with wholesome discipline; but, as a general thing, its effect is the reverse of this. In fine, the parental instinct is at once a safeguard and a stimulus: it both prompts and tempers the exercise of authority. God never would have instituted the relation without the instinct. His own love is paternal; and hence we feel, both that he cannot be tyrannical, and that he will not suffer our sins to go uncorrected. Whom the *Father* loveth he *chasteneth;* and there is the relation and the method, or at least the pattern, of the earthly parent.

CHAPTER XIV.

Respect to Parents.—History of an Undutiful Son.—Another Instance.—An Affectionate Granddaughter.—Fraternal Love.—Respect for Age.

My mother made it an object early to secure our *respect*, *confidence*, and *love*. She was always pleasant with her children, affectionate, accessible, sometimes playful, but never trifling. She did not *pet* them. Observing the way in which a young mother petted and *teased* her little daughter, "Ah!" said she, "she will have trouble with that child."

Respect to parents she so impressed upon us, by the propriety of the thing, by reference to Scripture, by its natural and its promised rewards, and by the calamitous consequences that were certain to follow filial disrespect, that there was no sin the thought of which was more shocking to us. I stood amazed, one day, to hear a young man using very disrespectful and abusive language to his mother; he even went so far as to curse her. "He will never prosper," said my mother, when I spoke of it to her; adding, and bidding me remember it, that she never knew son or daughter prosper that was unkind to parents. 'How *can* he prosper? Such a son has not the qualities in himself that are essential to prosperity and happiness. He that violates the first and most sacred of his relations, is of course prepared to violate all others. A bad son, he will be a bad brother, a bad husband, a bad neighbor, a bad citizen; and he that makes himself unworthy of these relations cannot but find himself uncomfortable in all human society. His unfilial conduct, if persisted in, is of itself sufficient to blast his character and prospects. It is shockingly unnatural. Men cannot respect him; he cannot respect himself. And then, the sin is so marked with the displeasure of God!" Thus she reasoned on this particular case. And all this was verified, as I lived to see, in the young man's experience. He did *not* prosper. He *might* have prospered: his prospects were good. He had fine features, and a robust and commanding person, native good sense, and even manly sentiments and generous impulses. His family was respectable, and he inherited considerable propĕrty. He was not addicted to any vice. But he was undutiful as a son, and that fact shaped his character and destiny. After the decease of his parents, he still proved a turbulent and oppressive brother to his four or five defenceless sisters; and set all law at defiance as a citizen and neighbor. He thought to go through the world as he had done through his family, with a high hand; the consequence of which was, that by and by he found himself pretty generally forsaken, shunned, and let alone. The world is too big for a single will to conquer.

God can find means to curb the sinner, and often does so in a quarter where he least looks for it. It was fit that he who had been the troubler of his father's house should receive his severest punishment in his own. He married a wife whom he loved with all his natural force of character; and he whose maxim and whose boast it was, never to be crossed in any thing—never to *submit* to any human will or law, however reasonable, found his match in his bosom companion. Of a quiet manner, and retired habits, she too had an indomitable will; and a perseverance in her temper which years could not exhaust. She knew his love for her, and her power over him through

AN UNDUTIFUL SON. 169

that medium. Samson's wife was not the last of the Delilahs. She knew the turbulence of his will, and that time would make him tire of its ebullitions and excitements. They had children, and he loved them also, with characteristic vehemence; and in them the mother had a new source of power: she attached them to her cause. At last, after years of humiliation and defeat, he could endure it no longer. He retired to a lone barn, fitted up a room in a corner of it, and there lived in solitude; was taken sick; returned home, and breathed out his vexed soul in the presence of his relenting wife and children, pitied by every body, mourned by none.

Such was the course and end of one who abused and cursed his mother. Let undutiful children mark such instances. Loss of fair prospects, and loss of love; vexatious litigation, and loss of property; years of domestic strife; disrespect from his own children; and finally a home among his cattle, with whom his whole life had shown him most *fit* to live—all these things were the direct and evident consequences of that one sin of disrespect to parents.

I trust that your own children, under the happy

influence of their parents, will be patterns of filial love and duty; and that it needs not the aid of such melancholy examples as this which I have given, to confirm them in that virtue. However, examples are impressive; and I shall not disoblige your children if I mention another case, of which my mother gave me the history, so far as it had then transpired, when I was young. It runs through three generations. A certain man, possessing one of the best houses, and one of the largest farms in the place, had three sons just grown up and married. He had already assisted them with property sufficient to enable them to live and thrive very well, with proper industry; and he proposed to divide his estate equally between them at his death. With a view to this, he had deeds prepared and executed—signed and sealed, but not delivered. He laid them away in his desk: they were of no validity as yet, because they were retained in his own hands, and were not put on the town records. He preferred this method to making a will, having perhaps that irrational aversion to making such an instrument which some people have, appearing to be superstitious about it, as if it presaged their death.

EJECTMENT OF THEIR PARENTS. 171

The sons, eager to anticipate the inheritance, broke open the desk, got possession of the deeds, and had them recorded. And now they were valid. Whether the father might have proved the fraudulency of the measure, and so made it null and void, I do not know; he did not do it; and so the property stood as legally theirs.

Their next step, at which they did not long hesitate, was to eject him, and take possession. They compelled their father and mother, now considerably in years, to retire to an old decayed house, on a solitary road, away from neighbors, and almost in the shade of a gloomy forest. There they spent the rest of their days, sorrowful, lone, and poor—they who had been so affluent; and the worst of their affliction was, to think of the ingratitude of their children. So solitary was the house, that squirrels made their nests in it, and were quite welcome to the aged pair, as their gambols sometimes diverted them from their sorrow. Birds also built their nests about them, quite familiarly, and reared their young, without experiencing such ungrateful returns from their offspring as they experienced from theirs.

The sons supplied them with the necessaries of

life for a while, but soon, as might be expected from such unnatural children, began to neglect and leave them to want. A man passing by, one day, and observing that all was still like the Sabbath, looked in at a window. He saw the old gentleman sitting alone, with his face in his hands, weeping; and asking the cause, "I am hungry," he replied, "and have nothing to eat."

The eldest son occupied the paternal mansion. There he lived in plenty. He had a little daughter, Grace. She was old enough to understand something of the wrong that had been done, and to feel pity for her grandparents. As often as she could she would go to see them, and would carry them some little thing for their comfort, if it were only a couple of eggs taken from the nest, or a bit of cake. She did not feel that this was stealing, for she knew that the property rightfully belonged to them, and that she was but giving them their own. One day her grandfather came to the house, and asked for a little vinegar. "I will draw it for you, grandpa'," said Grace, taking the jug from his hand, and running down cellar. Instead of vinegar, she filled it with molasses; and was in great fear lest her parents should find it out. So, to hasten her grandfather, she snatched her bonnet, saying she would go with him a part of the way, and carry the jug. She did so, and we may well believe that the act afforded her grandparents a hundred-fold more pleasure than the molasses.

But how did those sons prosper? I do not know their history minutely, but in brief it was this: one of them, while yet in the bloom of life, fell through the ice and was drowned, his wife witnessing the calamitous event. Another, the father of Grace, soon run through with his property, and died poor. The third suffered disgrace and mortification in the conduct of one of his daughters. He kept his property while he lived, and bequeathed it all to a selfish and prodigal only son. Then, in consequence of the will, came bitter contentions between that son and his sisters; and the widow was left to shift for herself, by them all. While the son built him a grand house, and flourished away, the poor mother pined in poverty, and used actually to pass by his door, and come to my parents for assistance. In the behavior of her children she reaped the natural fruits of the like behavior of the man she married, and whose wife she was at the time of his unfilial conduct towards her parents-in-law, without, perhaps, opposing it. Her son, after a very few years, became bankrupt both in property and in character, fled "between two days," went West, dragged out a miserable life there, and finally died a sot.

Few of the descendants of those three men have, so far as I know, been prospered. With a number of the third generation I was personally acquainted. It would be painful to describe the character and end of some of them. The sea swallowed up three of them. The iniquities of the fathers appear to have been visited upon the children unto the third generation; of the fourth, I have no knowledge.

But GRACE is an exception. She married into a respectable and pious family, has never wanted any good thing, and now (for she is still living, at a very venerable age) is amply and affectionately provided for in the family of a pious and wealthy daughter. More than all, she lives in hope of the glory of God, having early in life professed faith in Christ. Thus God has remembered her tenderness to her grandparents. And I dare say she was to her own parents a better daughter than they had reason to expect.

Honor thy father and mother (which is the first command with promise), that it may be well with thee, and that thou mayest live long on the earth.

On filial love hangs fraternal. Children that do not love their parents do not love each other. Indeed, all the sentiments proper to kindred and affinity are so blent and intertwined that one cannot suffer without injury to the others. Nothing would give our mother more concern than contention among her children; and I think our regard for her was one of the strongest motives with us to prevent it. I remember the first and last quarrel between myself and brother, and I remember, in connection with it, a mother's astonishment and grief, and the chastisement inflicted by our father, at her desire; and how well my conscience seconded both the reproof and the correction.

With respect for parents is coupled also respect for age, and for superiors generally. Honor thy father and thy mother, and, Thou shalt rise up before the hoary head, and honor the face of the old man, are precepts which generally stand or fall together. I do not forget the reproof I once received with reference to the latter. An old lady, a plain and unpretending, but very respectable woman, being at a house whither I was sent, on horseback, to do an errand, desired me to take her up behind me and help her homewards. I did so very readily, though I could not help feeling, being a small boy, that we made a rather awkward figure. At the parting of our roads, half a mile from her house, she proposed to get down and walk the rest, and I suffered her to do so, without objection. "But why did you not take her quite to her own door?" asked my mother. "Because she was an old woman, mother, and I did not care to." "Oh, yes!" she continued, "and for that very reason you should have done it. If it had been some spruce young girl you would have been pleased to take her all the way, but because she was old, you set her down. A young girl could have run home on her feet with ease and pleasure, but to her it was fatiguing. I am sorry your sense of propriety did not teach you better. Never again let *age* be a reason with you for neglect.

CHAPTER XV.

Discrimination with Respect to the Faults of Children.—Bees.—Injustice done to the Feelings and Behavior of Children.—Mrs. Howitt's Elephant —Plea in behalf of Little People.

In the discipline of children, as in all government, it is important to estimate offences according to the degree of their *moral obliquity*. Sins of ignorance, or of inadvertency, of which children commit a great many, are not to be put upon a par with deliberate and downright iniquities—even though the former be more mischievous in their effects (putting *moral* tendencies out of view) than the latter. This is very obvious, but not always acted on. There are parents who will be more disturbed by an accident than by a crime. For instance, they will more severely reprove or punish a child for breaking a looking-glass, or a piece of porcelain, than for a falsehood, or a quarrel. And what wonder if the child himself learns to estimate his conduct by the same law. An accident alarms him for the consequences, while a moral fault does not distress his conscience. So much *harm* done, so much *guilt;* or rather, so much obnoxiousness to punishment, or blame. An unsuccessful fraud, a lie from which no mischief follows, a fit of anger that injures nobody, is passed over by the parent as though it were venial; and so the child's conscience, as well as his fears, is relieved. Nor is that the worst. His conscience is *mis-instructed.* His moral vision is perverted, and a false standard of accountability and character given him, to take along with him up to manhood, and through life,—till the great tribunal of another world sets him right.

You will often see a child attempt to forestall the punishment of an act by offering the parent an equivalent. "How much did the broken thing cost? I will pay you for it out of the money I have got laid up." If the act was one of mere heedlessness, and if such heedlessness was habitual, it might be expedient to take the money, as a means of correcting the heedless habit. The heedlessness of servants is often corrected in this way. But suppose the fault were one of a *moral* nature, it would be monstrous to talk of an equivalent. There is no equivalent for the smallest sin, but in the merits of Christ—a fact which ought to be early and thoroughly impressed upon every mind. And yet, if we show ourselves more disquieted by the mischiefs that result from an act of heedlessness or ignorance than by the naked fact of a sinful act, or feeling, we seem to adopt the rule of measuring crime by equivalents. We teach our children so. It is the visible and computable *effects* of conduct, and not its *moral nature,* that we teach them to regard.

My mother never confounded the venial with the culpable; and I remember instances where, but for such discrimination in her, I might have smarted for doings that only incurred some gentle reproof, as a caution for the future. To give you an example. A cousin having come to see us, my brother and me, one summer day, we amused ourselves a while with observing the bees. The wish arose in our hearts that we had some of their honey. But how to get at it? At length it was suggested that, if a hive were overturned, they would fly away and leave their treasure at our mercy. "Who will upset it, then?" We were all quite young, myself the youngest; and as it generally happens among children that the risks and responsibilities are put upon the youngest, it was proposed to me to perform the feat. I got behind a hive, therefore, and over it went; and you may imagine the music about our ears that ensued thereupon. It was we that flew away, and not the bees. My mother came out, exclaiming at the hazard and the mischief, and, quite contrary to our expectation, said no more about it. Our very ignorance of the risk we ran (for we might have been stung to death) was evidence to her that we had no culpable intentions. She had the courage to replace the hive, greatly to the contentment of the bees, and had the good fortune to do so without getting stung. Do you know that bees have a special antipathy to some people, and will sting them almost unprovoked, while others can do any thing with them with impunity? She was one of their favorites, as they were hers.

I apprehend that we often do injustice to the feelings and behavior of children by not duly considering that they *are* children. We forget how inexperienced they are, how excitable, how imaginative, and impulsive. A friend of ours, in a letter, the other day, described the high excitement of her little daughter, whom she was about to take with her on a visit to some relations. The child ran up stairs and down, flew to the window, as if to anticipate the carriage, and could neither eat nor sleep. "Is it possible," exclaims the mother, "that *I* was ever such an one?" Yes, madam, you were, probably, very much such an one.

Mrs. Howitt, in her "Own Story," tells us that in her childhood she saw on a distant hill-top what seemed to her "an immense elephant, or monstrous beast. I never saw it as any thing else," she says. "I was not at all afraid of it, for I saw it every day. Once I said to a visitor, when in a very talkative humor, that a great black elephant always stood opposite to our house. My parents reproved me for saying that which was not true. I stoutly maintained that it was so; my firmness seemed like willful obstinacy, and I was reproved severely; but I would not withdraw my assertion, and my parents, grieving to see such perversity, thought it much better to let the subject drop. This affair sunk deep in my mind. I saw the elephant every day as plain as could be, but I dared not recur to the subject, because it had given so much displeasure. The fields, however, were bought; and then we went to the very top of them; and as I ascended the hill, my elephant was gone, there was nothing at all but two dark Scotch firs, and a slender ash tree growing beside them. [The trunks and tops of the firs forming the legs and body of the creature, and the ash the head and proboscis, aided by the obscurity of the English atmosphere, which is much less clear than ours.] The whole thing was disenchanted; and when I returned home, though I still, by a stretch of the imagination, could see the elephant, it gradually became three distinct trees. I never, as I remember, mentioned it to any one, not even to Anna, but it made a deep impression on my mind, and has given me great charity with the exaggerations and even the apparent falsehoods of children."

Truth, strict truth, is certainly to be inculcated. The slightest deviations from it should alarm us, and put us upon correcting so pernicious a habit. There can be no true excellence of character— there is no foundation for it, without integrity. Behold an Israelite indeed, in whom is *no guile*. Even the honest exaggerations of a lively imagination ought to be checked, lest they lead to something worse. Yet, mere misapprehensions, elephants made out of trees, are not to be treated as wilful whole-cloth falsehoods.

When I see how very strict and strait-laced some people are with children, I feel disposed to put in a plea or two in their behalf. Pray be a little tolerant of our mirth and noise, because of the excess of our animal spirits; which we can no more repress wholly than you can stop the gushing fountains and flowing brooks of Spring. How delightful to all young creatures is freedom! Pray suffer us to breathe a little of that wholesome luxury. Why should we be made to envy the lambs that frolic in the pastures? What! is our home a monastery, and are we monks and nuns, that *nowhere* and *never* can we for a moment seem to ourselves exempt from irksome supervision—never feel ourselves at large a little, to run about as our eager senses and our sportive spirits prompt us? How absurd to say to us, as you often do in look and in effect, if not in just those words, "Don't be so childish!" What are we else but children, and what else is to be expected but that we should think as children, speak as children, and understand, and act as children? When we become men and women we shall behave as such. You wonder at our emotions and behavior; you see nothing to justify it. We are always looking, hearkening, shouting, leaping, wishing, fearing, hoping, in the midst of the most ordinary objects. Well, we have to say to you that the most ordinary things are new and strange to us, and therefore exciting. Do but consider that that mountain there—hill or hillock only, as it may seem to you—over which the blue sky sleeps, or the fleecy clouds sail, is the first, perhaps the only like elevation we ever saw, and saw that so recently that it does not yet cease to affect us with a feeling of the sublime. To you it is a fixed and motionless object; but to us its top nods and swims, as if it were going to topple down, or sail away. High trees, tall steeples, great rocks, deep pits and gullies, dark fathomless wells, frightful precipices, awful solitudes, great storms and floods, roaring winds and cataracts, loud thunder, lightnings that can be felt upon the hands and face, unutterable splendors in the rainbow—these and such like things, how few of them you seem to perceive at your time of life; but we, all sensitive, and wakeful, and inexperienced as we are, are meeting with them continually. We see a thousand sights you do not

see, and hear a thousand sounds you do not hear.
How alive to us the air is with birds; how social
the woods with winged creatures, quadrupeds, and
creeping things. A squirrel arrests and amuses
us as a mastodon would hardly arrest you. What
an incident to us is the passage of the wild-geese
screaming along their airy way mid-heaven! Do
you see how vexed the sunbeams are with insects?
You heed them not; you even brush them from
your eyes and breath with scarce a consciousness
of their presence. What a saucy rogue is echo!
How startling is the sudden singing of the locust;
and what a din the beetle makes upon the wing!
What mysterious things the fireflies are, twinkling in the dark; and how wakeful does the distant baying of the mastiff keep us, when we have
gone to bed! A love of the marvelous we confess. It is natural alike to us and you, with this
difference, that with you experience has done
away with the objects that used to excite it.

Some such plea as this I incline to make in behalf of such little people as are subjected to uncharitable judgment, or over-strict restraint. A
still child is either unwell or unnatural; and a
child that sees things with the senses of an adult

is either a prodigy or a dolt. The eyes of children are magnifying lenses, and their ears acoustic tubes. They see things large and wonderful, and see them manifold and multiform—a hundred cats where there are but two or three. Hence the cumulative style of their descriptions—"great, big, large"—with all the other intensive words and synonyms they are able to command; and hence we often charge them, and sometimes cruelly, perhaps, with culpable exaggerations, if not with downright falsehoods, when they do but report things as they apprehend them. Hyperbole with them is not hyperbole, in all cases. Do we not all naturally use such language as our senses and emotions dictate? And who shall acquit us grown people of expressing more, or expressing less, than the truth, if other people's senses and experience are to be the standard?

An intelligent gentleman, who had been absent above fifty years from his and our native place, requested my brother to conduct him to the "Beggar-land." This was a little common, a rood or more of green-sward, elliptical in form, with a bank round its sides. It had been a favorite playground of several generations. On coming to the spot, "*That* the Beggar-land!" he exclaimed. "But how extravagant were my impressions of it! carried away with me in my childhood. I imagined those banks to be at least seventy feet high, and would almost have taken my oath of it; whereas they are not above a dozen feet. And they cannot but be as high now as they ever were, indeed they must be higher; for the level turf is as it was, while the road on one side and the little water-course on the other would naturally be wearing deeper, and thus increase the elevation between."

Thus we see things in our childhood; and due allowance should be made for it, in justice and in charity. However, these remarks must not be pushed too far. While we teach the heart to *mean* truth, we should also discipline the senses to *perceive* the truth; that so the heart, the senses, and the tongue, may all be truthful. How amiable is truthfulness, how beautiful is truth!

CHAPTER XVI.

Restraint and Freedom.—Effects of Excessive Supervision.—Our Mother's Course.—Attempt at Reaping.—Society and Companionship.—Acquaintance with the World.

OVERSIGHT and restraint there must be, certainly. Young life is too exuberant not to need pruning; too rampant not to require training and keeping-in. Yet restraint should not be too rigorous. Besides that the sense of freedom is one of the most delightful feelings to the child, and to the man, it is favorable to virtue, and ought for that reason to be allowed within all safe and wholesome limits. Many an instance of concealment, falsehood, truantship, obduracy, and eventual lawlessness, has been owing to an over-stringent domestic supervision; though I do not doubt that the far more common origin of such mischiefs is a too great *laxness* of supervision. If I were not talking to a woman of sense and prudence, I should hardly dare to say some things that I do. There is a medium between austerity and laxness, and between servitude and licentiousness, which you will easily discern. Liberty itself, true liberty, is a medium condition; and such liberty is favorable to virtue, while slavery is its blight, as all history shows. Just now the nations are throwing off the shackles of their old feudal despotisms, and proclaiming liberty; and we look for their corresponding advancement in intelligence and moral worth. A degree of licentiousness may be the first effect; but if licentiousness gives scope and currency to vice for a time, despotism begets, nurses, and perpetuates it.

A too minute and constant supervision not only tries the temper of the child, but is unfavorable to the formation of a strong and useful character. If you direct him in every effort, call him back from every ramble, question every absence from your sight, apprise him of every little danger, contrive all his amusements for him, in a word, if you keep him every moment in leading strings and tethers, you will make a feeble and dependent creature of him. An English writer says, he was once present when an old mother, who had brought up a large family with eminent success, was asked by a young one what she would recommend in the case of some children who were too anxiously educated, and her reply was, "I think, my dear, a little wholesome neglect." Much must be left to the spontaneous impulses of the child's nature—to his natural love of achievement and of self-reliance and self-approbation, to his conscious bravery, his instinct of self-preservation, and the teachings of experience. Much also must be left to the *providence of God.* Do we forget that our heavenly Father unites with us in caring for our children; and with an eye that never is averted from them, and never sleeps? It is a needful relief of mind to commit them to his keeping; and, moreover, it is hardly to be doubted that *excessive* anxiety about the lives and limbs of children, amounting, as it often does, to a sinful distrust, or non-recognition, of his care, is often rebuked by their being taken away. I remember my mother alluding to this, and mentioning the following fact. A mother at meeting on Sunday recollected a tub of water into which her little child might fall and be drowned. The thought gave her so much uneasiness that she could not attend to the services. She left the house and went home. The child was safe and well in the care of the person that had been intrusted with it. She took a book, therefore, and sat down to read; but by and by, missing her child, she went to look for it, and found it drowned in the tub.

It is only by some measure of such "wholesome neglect" that the natural manliness of the boy, and the womanly consciousness of the girl, can grow up to their proper adult force and value.

The same is true with regard to their *moral*, as well as their physical training. I think it very possible to over-do in our attention to the moral behavior of our children; though I must repeat that under-doing is by far the more common fault. And I am aware how delicate it is to speak of over-doing. How *can* we do too much, or be too careful, on that head, will many be ready to ask; while others will adopt the suggestion as a cover to their negligence. However, there is a medium in this matter, as in every other, where wisdom is profitable to direct, and if deviation to the right of the line, as well as to the left, be mischievous, it is well to be aware of it. Whether to the left lies the greater mischief, and the more common tendency, is not the question; but whether deviation to the right be possible, or mischievous at all.

While, then, I do by no means advocate laxness of supervision, or connivance at childish sins, I apprehend that an extremely minute and anxious scrutiny kept up always, a strict account taken, and on the spot, of every childish indiscretion, or childish word, or action, a perpetual lecturing the child about his behavior, in however severe or gentle tones, a continual warning him against the lesser and ordinary, as well as the grosser and more baleful evils, of the living world around him, and against himself, may be indiscreet and harmful in various ways. The mischief may be less or greater, and may be various, according to the natural temper of the child. The effect may be to vex and harass the spirit till it bolts from all restraint, through very weariness of *surveillance*, precept, and reproof. Or you may induce an extreme scrupulosity—a timid and morbid apprehension of wrong-doing instead of a direct and liberal aim at right-doing. There is a certain high-minded integrity which, almost unreflecting and unconscious, and not less the result of discipline, is equally averse from sinning, and more safe, than a conscience *servilely* subjected to duty. Moral freedom is an essential attribute of moral agency;

God has endowed us with it: and the consciousness of such freedom, as well as of the responsibility connected with it, ought not to be impaired, but cherished. Nothing is more amiable and hopeful than a teachable and tender conscience in a child; but a conscience reduced to a mere negative passivity, and that has no moral courage, a vague, precocious, *coward* conscience (if I may use such an expression), a conscience of forced growth and unnatural sensibility, is no guaranty for moral soundness at a more advanced stage of life. Such children have often been known to grow up to great heartlessness and hardness. "The conscience of a child," says the writer before quoted, "may easily be worn out, both by too much pressure, and by over-stimulation. I have known a child to have a conscience of such extraordinary and premature sensibility, that at seven years of age she would be made ill by remorse for a small fault. She was brought up by persons of excellent understanding, with infinite care and affection, and yet by the time she was twenty years of age, she had next to no conscience, and a hard heart."*

* Notes from Life, by Henry Taylor.

Or, finally, the effect of such incessant and minute attention may be to destroy the child's simplicity. In thus occupying him with his faults, or with his virtues, you occupy him with *himself;* and the danger is, that so you will make him an egotist, or a pharisee, or both. Why should he not be egotistical and selfish, when he finds himself made the centre of all your and his attentions? The objects that produce and exercise goodness, like the objects that excite and exercise faith, lie beyond us, and we must go out of ourselves to feel their influence; and it seems an unhopeful way to make the child good by merely talking to him about goodness, as a quality in him—by merely saying to him continually, "you must be *so,* and not *so*"—as it is to make a man a believer by merely talking to him of faith. We must engage and exercise him in actual well-doing, and the more we can do this through his own unthought-of, or at least untalked-of, impulses and convictions, the better. The amiable and proper, and the safe state of feeling, in regard to behavior—in morals as in manners—is the same as that we inculcate respecting dress: to wear it

MY MOTHER'S COURSE. 195

without consciousness. See that it be proper and becoming, and think no more about it.

In fine, much must be left to the child's moral sense, properly instructed; to his enlightened and instinctive apprehension of the consequences of transgression; to the silent force of example; to experience and time; to the influence of prayer; and to God's providence and Spirit.

As for *us*, we did not feel our young life to be a condition either of unrestricted liberty or of irksome bondage. A wholesome restraint was exercised, and, at the same time, a wholesome freedom allowed. As to *life and limb*, I think our father was more apt to be apprehensive that mischief might befall us than our mother was: but it was not in his nature to mar our pleasure by unnecessary restrictions. She commended us to God, and endeavored to dismiss all unprofitable solicitude about us. She often left us at large, to ramble heedless and afar, in our pastimes (and indeed so did he), to a degree, and with a composure that now surprises me. I often think that were *my* boys to incur half the "disastrous chances, and moving accidents by flood and field, and hairbreadth 'scapes," that my brother and I did, in our boyhood, I should be in continual uneasiness. She may have felt more anxiety at times, and probably did, than she expressed.

She was not afraid of heat or cold, or storm or hardship for us, especially for her boys: she took good care of us if we were sick, which was seldom, and for the rest, taught us not to mind trifles. One day in harvest, for example, while the men were at their dinner, I thought it a good time to try my hand at reaping; and with the first clip with the sharp and ragged sickle, split my little finger lengthwise, nearly severing one half of it from the other, and spoiling one of the joints. My mother bound it up, for she was our surgeon as well as nurse; and it happening at that moment that a boy was wanted to ride ten miles to fetch a horse back, she proposed that I should go. "Never mind the finger," said she; "the ride will divert you from the aching of it, and you will see places and things that will be new to you." I was put up behind the man, therefore, with one well hand to manage with, and was much diverted by the journey. I had never traveled half so far alone. One object, especially, which I saw, and had to

MORAL CARE. 197

tell of when I got home, filled my imagination, and impressed me very deeply with the hardness of the transgressor's way, namely, a gloomy old jail, the first I had ever seen. Not long before (which served to increase the force of my impressions), my father had sat on a jury which had brought in their painful and awful verdict of "guilty" of murder, against a prisoner there confined. He was hung.

The scar of that sickle-cut remains, and is permanently associated with the pitiful and yet cheering look of my mother binding up the finger of her boy. Never mind the finger.

Her *moral* care of us was qualified with the same largeness of mind. I think, and can testify for her, that she conscientiously endeavored to fulfil, and did in fact fulfil in a good degree, that injunction in Deut. vi. 6–9. She was a diligent teacher of religious truth and duty. But she did not deem it expedient to be urging the subject of religion on us directly and personally every moment, or think that the amount of impression would correspond with the amount of talk, which is the unfortunate idea of some good people. Never a day passed, I presume, without more or less of instruction or suggestion from her, on serious subjects; she dropped words, improved incidents, availed herself of favorable opportunities, and at times talked to us in the most direct and earnest manner.

One of the greatest moral dangers to which children and youth are exposed, I think the greatest, is evil companions; and I remember a time when my mother felt and manifested a good deal of concern on my own account from this cause, with reference to a particular family. They were very respectable in point of property, and the sons had those bold and hardy qualities which are apt to excite the admiration of their fellows: but they were very corrupt. *"So shall your children make our children cease from fearing the Lord."* From the intercourse of decidedly corrupt companions, be their pretensions what they may, we must by all means separate our children, as we would not see them ruined. But to separate them from all such society, or intercourse, as is not just what we could wish, is not possible, unless we would seclude them from all contact with the world at large, which is worse than the evil sought to be shunned. I knew a family brought up in this policy. The parents were excellent people, but of strict notions and retired habits. The children went to the public school, but went and came as straight as possible, never mixing with their mates there or elsewhere. I cannot say much for the results. They were all moral, and some of them pious; but were all sadly ignorant of men. They thought worse of them than they ought to think. This was natural; for what to them was the meaning of their seclusion thus from all human intercourse, but that human kind were too corrupt for them to mingle with? The daughters were inoffensive, retired women. Of the sons, one, converted in middle life, was and is a much-respected, worthy man, but a rather uncomfortable member of society, being stoutly, but honestly, on the *offside* of almost any public measure—a resolute and fixed minority, with perhaps the entire parish against him. Not to distrust the views and motives of the many, and keep aloof from them, would be inconsistent with the sentiments in which he was educated. Another of them, moral, but not pious, whom I knew only as a man in middle life, was the most distrustful of all the world, and of all the world's doings, that you can conceive of, much to his discomfort, and somewhat, too, to the discomfort of others; for it was distressing, as well as amusing, to see what bugbears possessed him at every movement of the day. A turnpike or a toll-gate, for example, was a monopoly that tended directly and most surely to the moneyed aggrandizement of a class, and so to an aristocracy, and so to the subversion of the republic; while the republic itself, with its suffrages in so many wicked hands, portended any thing but good.

With the world, such as it is, our children *must* mix, more or less; nor is it desirable, if it be possible, to prevent it. It is a calamity to a child to live and grow up *alone*—whether in the midst of society, or in "a wild unknown to public view." From the companionship of the particularly corrupt we must preserve them; but as for the rest, the best we can do is, to counteract the evil by faithful and timely counsels, by our own example, by early acquainting them with the virtuous and good, and by prayer. So prayed our Saviour for his disciples; and for you and me also, and for our children, if we are his. "I pray not that thou shouldst take them out of the world, but that thou shouldst keep them from the evil. Neither pray I for these alone; but for them also which shall believe on me through their word." The fact is, our children are moral agents, like ourselves, and under moral trial. Good and evil are before them, and they have power to choose. God so wills it. It is in such circumstances that they have to form, and only *can* form, a moral character; for without trial, character is nominal. We may, by secluding them from all contact with the world while they are young, *postpone* the trial; but we cannot finally avert it. Sooner or later, if they live, they will have to experience the probation which God intends for all. If early and gradually inured to it, they will be likely to endure the conflict unharmed, and more than that, established and increased in virtue. But if they meet it inexperienced, they will meet it with but the skill and power of moral weaklings, and with doubtful issue. More than this, they have important duties to perform, as Christ's servants, in and towards the world, and they must know the world to be qualified to act in it

CHAPTER XVII.

Commendation and Reproof

Some ladies were conversing with my mother about their and her children. Being in the next room, I overheard one of them remark concerning myself, that she thought, from what she had observed of me, I was a truthful child. "He *is* an honest boy," my mother replied. "I do not think he ever deceived, or told a lie." The remark arrested and surprised me; for though I knew that falsehood deserved *reproof*, it had not occurred to me that truth was a subject for *commendation*. I had supposed that truth was to be spoken *of course*, without any thought of its meriting or receiving praise. However, the commendation gratified me, and (for I distinctly remember my consciousness, though very young at the time) without elating me, or exciting the least vanity. The feeling was that of a virtuous self-approbation, or self-respect. It was a new *sense of character*, and it served to *confirm* me in the commended habit of truthfulness. And if from that day to this I never have (as I hope I have not) uttered a conscious falsehood, I am no doubt much indebted to that conversation for it.

I refer to the incident here as suggesting generally, the wisdom of employing judicious commendation as a means of encouraging the young in good behavior, as well as reproof for correcting that which is bad. We think reproof needful, and use it freely; but are we not apt to think too little of the good effect of commendation also? Perhaps we fear that it will engender pride, or otherwise corrupt the motives; and there may be danger of this, if praise be indiscreetly given; or, perhaps, we say that virtue is to be practiced as being right and proper in itself, and that that is motive enough. True; but may we not give energy to that very motive of love and respect for virtue, instead of displacing it, by expressing our approbation of it in connection with the good behavior of the child?

Motives, I know, are delicate things to deal with; but they are to be dealt with nevertheless, not negatively, but positively. They hold a prominent place in the business of moral training, and are a most essential part of the self-knowledge which the child should be led as far as possible to acquire. And among the motives thus demanding attention is the desire of approbation; which, whether we will or no, exists in every bosom, and is not to be wisely disposed of by merely repressing, or letting it alone.

The love of approbation is natural; and if it be *natural*—if the Creator has implanted it in the human breast, has he not designed that it shall have its uses? In that delicate and wise combination of qualities comprised in the constitution of the human soul, we must suppose there are no superfluous ones. The desire in question, therefore, has its uses. And it *will have* its operation and effect, either in a right direction or in a wrong one. A French benevolent society,* having the care of juvenile delinquents consigned to it by the government, in one of its reports, speaking of the effect of commendation, and giving striking instances of individuals confirmed in hopeful courses by this means, remarks, "Man needs success, needs approval. How many, not being able to gain the plaudits of the good, have

* The Agricultural and Penitentiary Colony of Mettray.

gone to seek the approbation of the wicked! Too much cannot be done to develop noble and useful ambitions."

Does not every one—not children only, but older people, and not the vicious only, but the virtuous—feel the wholesome stimulus of commendation—of commendation not presumed merely, but *expressed?* Does not the wife feel it in the commendatory words and smiles with which the husband notices the neatness and comfort that are the result of her cares? How it invigorates her efforts, and mitigates her fatigue! Does not the mother feel it when some friend, observing her intelligent and well-behaved children, says, How well you have trained them? Is king or president above it? I think that our statesmen, the most disinterested and faithful in the world, would be better still if our parties and our presses would deal less in calumnies, and more in just acknowledgments of their merits. And the little child, in the school-room, every where, and most of all in the presence of his parents—how delightfully and impulsively does he feel the stimulus of favorable notice and merited commendation! How it incites him to further diligence, and to greater excellence! But, to have toiled at his little task (as we may think it, but herculean to him it may be), unnoticed in the process, and uncommended when it is done; to have done spontaneously a generous act; to have controlled his temper, kept still at church, or behaved well at home; and receive no mark of approbation for it, how discouraging! Or if he have not looked for such expressed approval, or thought of it beforehand, still it is not less encouraging to receive it.

Coming home from school one day, my mother said to me, "John, as I hear you are a good boy at school, and as you are a good boy at home, I have bought this book for you;" and she put into my hands "The Child's Instructor." There have been several books, I believe, with that title, but I have never seen one, nor a whole edition of them, of equal value with that one. I remember the shape and size of it, its gay exterior, its large type, not a word, however, of its contents—they may be still mingling in the general current of my thoughts, or may have been permanently dyed into my feelings; but I can never forget what I felt to be far more precious than the book itself—a mother's approbation.

To what, indirectly, do we appeal when we reprove a fault? To this same love of approbation. There would be no sensibility to reproof if there were no desire of approbation. The one implies the other. The sentiment appealed to being the same in both cases, therefore, it does not seem wise or *fair* to deal with it by halves—all blame and no praise—supposing both to be deserved.

As to the manner of expressing approbation, it may be various, only avoiding always such modes as may seem likely to excite vanity, or give a mercenary or selfish character to motives. It may be done by approving words, smiles, or rewards. You remember the anecdote of Benjamin West, whose mother kissed him for one of his earliest efforts with the pencil. "That kiss," said he, "made me a painter." Behold the life-directing, life-lasting power of a mother's kiss!

CHAPTER XVIII.

Physical Education, especially of Girls.—Young Life in the Country.—My Sisters.—Young Ladies on Horseback.—Apple Gathering.—Aeropathy.—Our Climate.

I HAVE alluded elsewhere briefly to our physical education. I must advert to it again, with special reference to the girls. In this country the physical education of sons is much better managed, or left to manage itself, so far as exercise is concerned, than that of daughters. Their out-door sports, if nothing else, tend to make them hardy. *We* were accustomed, through the summer, to the healthful industry of farming, an employment, both physically and morally regarded, more wholesome for boys than any other. Add to this our healthful rural pastimes—skating, sliding, the ball-ground, bathing, rowing and sailing, and the long amble through wild wood and prairie, and over hill and dale. For health and virtue's sake, for pure pleasure, and for the mind's sake, I would not fail to have spent my young life in the country for half the city's wealth.

"Hath not old custom made this life more sweet
Than that of painted pomp? Are not these woods
More free from peril than the envious court?

* * * * * *

And this our life, exempt from public haunt,
Finds tongues in trees, books in the running brooks,
Sermons in stones, and good in every thing."

"God made the country, and man made the town.
What wonder, then, that health and virtue, gifts
That can alone make sweet the bitter draught
That life holds out to all, should most abound
And least be threatened in the fields and groves?"

I can speak of my sisters in their childhood as excellent specimens of health, activity, and bloom. They had healthy parents, it is true, and inherited sound constitutions; but I attribute their vigor still more to the *habits* in which their mother allowed and encouraged them. Besides that they were trained to be industrious and useful in the house, which is so promotive of the health of daughters, as well as essential to their future competency as housekeepers—qualities, be it remembered, which the piano, and the ball-room, nor any mere fashionable accomplishments can supply—they were accustomed to take a large share of their recreations in the open air. I remember many a cheerful ramble with them, many an excursion after nuts and berries, many a play at hide-and-seek. The best, perhaps, of all Poor Richard's maxims, "Early to bed, and early to rise," was practiced by them, and by us all. How pestiferous to health, efficiency, good temper, and good morals, is late lying in bed—a habit which must be corrected before it is formed, to wit, in youth, or it never will be. I do not say in childhood; for little children, like the lark and the robin, are naturally early risers. Keep up, if possible, the practice through the teens, and the habit is established. What a shame, and how prognostic of sloth and mediocrity, or worse, in any house, is son or daughter on whom the morning sun habitually "looks down and says, Inglorious here he lies!"

They went a long way to school, always on their feet, in all weathers, except the roughest—an exercise which counteracted, in some degree, the unhealthful effect of the six hours' confinement, impure air, dust, and study of the school-room. Those hours are too many, by one third, for young frames and minds, the world will one day think, and will abridge them. There is the origin of many a curved spine, deranged nervous system, and injured constitution, especially in females. I must not forget to say they were early accustomed to the side-saddle, and were excellent equestrians —an exercise so healthful and becoming to young ladies, that, for their sakes, I could almost wish that wheels had never been thought of. But I dislike the *trappings* with which they now accompany the exercise, the length of their skirts being not only an inconvenience, but what is worse, an affectation. Our grandmothers used, in their blooming days, not only to gallop a mile, but to go long journeys on horseback, in their ordinary dresses. And then this dangling fashion discourages the general use of the exercise, inasmuch as many a sensible girl is averse both to the expense and the display of so much cloth and feathers.

I will mention another thing. Those were cider-making days; we had a wide waste of orchards, scattered here and there about the farm, on the slopes and hill-tops, and in the flats and valleys—showing like rural wealth, but really a *waste*, since the fruit was converted into cider, and the cider, much of it (not by us), into alcohol. Such was the practice of that day. There came, by the way, in time, a sweeping temperance agent, in the shape of a mighty wind, which laid those orchards prostrate, few of the trees surviving it. This was years in advance of the temperance society, and I wish from my heart it had occurred much earlier. It was a great work to gather so many apples, and my sisters were often sent, along with their brothers, to assist—Michael Bruin being of the party, generally, to empty baskets and look after us. You will think this an unfeminine employment, perhaps, and my sisters might not thank me for mentioning it; but I can assure you they never seem to me so blooming and comely as when I think of them with their faces glowing beneath their sun-bonnets in those orchards, breathing the autumn air, with an autumn sky above them. They were never employed at *haymaking*, as you see young ladies in an English picture, and as I have seen in fact—not *peasant* girls, but young *ladies*—and wished the example followed on our side of the water! That picture is a pleasing one; and could you see the group we apple-gatherers made, with our industry and playfulness, and our baskets proportioned to our sizes, and Bruin, in his wonted humor towards us, shaking down from some well-loaded limb an unexpected and astounding shower of apples on our hats and bonnets, you would, perhaps, confess the picture not unworthy of a place with that of the rakes and pitchforks. The girls did no other out-door work, with the exception of weeding flowers.

You have daughters, Mrs. ——; pray do not be afraid of the air for them: it is the best catholicon, the best cosmetic in the world. Send them out to ramble; contrive errands for them—"walks of *usefulness*"—if possible, which benefit the heart as well as the limbs; give them flowers and strawberries to weed, and shrubberies and vines to cultivate, and plants to water; let them, when old enough, learn something of the pleasant and useful art of pomology, and bud young fruit-trees in the garden; and if they *romp*, do not be scandalized, or alarmed for their gentleness and refinement; it is just as natural, just as healthful, just as *innocent* and *becoming* (whatever prejudice and custom may say) for young girls to run and shout, as it is for boys. In a word, accustom them early and habitually to all safe and wholesome atmospheric influences; and enjoin it on them to keep up such habits while they live: and when you have done so, you will have no cause to fear but, that under the influence of American custom, and of our climate of intensities—of burning heat and freezing cold, and saturating dews—they will, as they grow older, shrink quite enough for delicacy and femineness (and quite too much for health and efficiency) into the shades of their well-darkened parlors. Alas! for the confined in-door habits of our countrywomen. We have homœopathy, hydropathy, allopathy, idiopathy; when will our ladies understand that the best of all the *pathies* is *aeropathy?* An English mother scarcely thinks of dining till she has taken an airing, walking miles sometimes, with her daughters; and the most beautiful people that the world contains, as I believe, and apparently the most vivacious and cheerful, are the peasantry of Tuscany (I refer to the female peasantry particularly), who almost live in the open air. The peculiar cultivation of the country leads to this; consisting, to a great extent, of vineyards, olives, and the mulberry, in the light work of which females are employed. Their climate also is one of the finest.

Ours is *not* the finest; nor is it the worst.

Such as it is, we must use ourselves to it. De Tocqueville says that it is better, taking the country at large, than that of Europe. And yet, how much less are our women abroad, and how much less ruddy and vigorous than the European. While I think of this, I am made to fear for the health and vigor of my own sex, eventually, and so for the health and vigor of the nation. And let us remember that physical deterioration involves *mental* and *moral* deterioration. Look at the masses in English manufacturing towns, that are dwarfed in body, mind, and heart. True, health is not virtue, nor virtue health; but is it not largely true that the habits which are unfriendly to the one are unfavorable to the other?

> ' Good health, and, its associate in most,
> *Good temper;* spirits prompt to undertake,
> And not soon spent, though in an arduous task;
> The powers of fancy and strong thought are theirs."

Whose? The poet is speaking of "th' alert and active," in contrast with those who live in-door languor, indolence, and "love of rest."

CHAPTER XIX.

Constancy of Teaching and Impression.—Habitual Reference to the Bible.—Lessons from the Living World.—Society of the Good.—Nature and its Teachings.—The Flower Garden.—The Book of Providence.

My mother was fain to avail herself of whatever might be turned to the moral, or the mental benefit of her children. Every little incident, as well as larger occurrence, was to her purpose. Directly and indirectly, in a thousand ways, and often in ways scarcely observable by others, or conscious to herself, she sought to produce some salutary impression on their hearts, or lead them to some profitable reflection. There is something in this gentle *constancy* of teaching and impression that makes a mother's influence on the tender mind like the dew upon the grass. " Blessed are they that sow beside all waters." " In the morning sow thy seed, and in the evening withhold not thy hand: for thou knowest not whether shall prosper, either this or that, or whether they both shall be alike good. These passages she often quoted to herself as impulsive suggestions to duty, and as encouraging assurances of success. And she often quoted them to us also, as beautifully applicable to all well-doing—connecting desirable results with human diligence on the one hand, and God's providence on the other.

On all moral subjects, not to say on those of a temporal nature also, she referred us to the Bible. It was the exhaustless store-house of her counsels and their sanctions. In this way she led us to a *practical* acquaintance with the Holy Book, and taught us to regard it as at once our guide, monitor, and friend.

With regard to other books, if we had, or might have had, any disposition to read those of a frivolous character, or immoral tendency, she forestalled it by furnishing us with better. I never read but one immoral book in my life; and for the few pages I read by stealth in that, my conscience smote me so that I quit it.

From the living world around us she drew many a lesson. The example of the good she commended to our imitation, and warned us by the bad. Of these she spoke without severity, manifesting always pity and concern for them, and calling to mind that caveat against pharisaical self-esteem, Who maketh thee to differ? While she had none of that spurious charity which puts no difference between vice and virtue, truth and error, she was exceedingly averse to evil-speaking. I have seldom seen a person with equal discernment of character, and at the same time equal charity and forbearance.

She sought for us the society and the prayers of pious people; and taught us especially to respect and love our minister. That made his prayers impressive to us, his sermons attractive, his visits welcome, and his counsels weighty. The venerable man regarded us with a shepherd's love, and sympathized with her in her solicitude for us. In many an hour of difficulty—I will not say of discouragement, for a mind stayed on God, like hers, is never discouraged—he was her counselor and comforter; and often when he spoke to me on some matter touching my welfare, for this world or another, I could imagine some hint from her that led to it.

She possessed, in an unusual degree an unaffected, quiet, pure *love of nature*, and cultivated the same in us, to pleasurable and pious uses. It was a characteristic act in her—characteristic both of her love of flowers and her love of home—at the time of her marriage, to pull up a rose-tree and take it with her to her new residence, planting it under a window, where it long stood and flourished, and still stands, unless stranger hands have destroyed or removed it. It was a beautiful damask, and was a favorite and cherished thing among our shrubbery, not only for its beauty, but still more for its associations. We called it "Mother's rose." A root of it was transplanted to our new house, when we removed.

She loved the minute in nature, as well as the great, the beautiful as well as the sublime; and by associating all with the Creator, she felt her piety quickened, and her pleasure enhanced. In her, Cowper's lines were truly applicable.

> Happy who walks with Him! whom what he finds
> Of flavor, or of scent, in fruit or flower,
> Or what he views of beautiful or grand
> In nature, from the broad majestic oak
> To the green blade that twinkes in the sun,
> Prompts with remembrance of a present God.
> His presence, who made all so fair, perceived,
> Makes all still fairer.

She had a little inclosure devoted to flowers, shrubbery, and small fruit, and cultivated exclusively by her, with our willing, but sometimes mischievously unskillful hands to help. "Mother, is this a weed, or a flower, that I have pulled up?" I remember observing her in that garden, when I was a very little child, as she held a small flower which she had just gathered, and gazed at it in silence. Her eyes filled, and turning to me, she said, "See how beautiful!" and pointing out to me its exquisite tints, its delicate and fragile structure, and its fragrance, she added, "God made it. He only *could* make it. How wonderful is his skill!" That flower, and her comment on it, made an impression on my mind at once solemn, elevating, and indelible. I cast my young eyes around on the gay and fragrant blossoms that surrounded me, and felt that I was in the presence of the beautiful, the inimitable works of God—things which he made, and which he only could make. I could touch them, and take them in my hand! Why should we not all, and always, feel so, both in the familiar garden, and wherever God has wrought? Who reads of Eden in the Scriptures, or in Milton's description of it, or sees it in a

"See, How Beautiful!"

painting, without associating with it the divine presence and the divine skill? Why should we not endeavor to realize—how can we *help* realizing, the same presence, and the same hand, in every landscape and locality under heaven?

It was her habit thus to associate in our minds the Creator with his works; and this should be done by every parent. The book of nature is as truly the book of God as is his written word. It is full of the moral world, as the Bible is of the natural. It is full of God: day unto day uttereth speech, and night unto night showeth knowledge of him, through this medium. The psalmist, in the nineteenth psalm, has, with admiration equally devout, celebrated both these volumes connectedly, and he shows in many of his writings alike the habit of his own mind, and what ought to be the habit of all.

How full of speaking facts and images, how suggestive of elevated thought, how productive of pure and pleasing emotions, does the *poet* find this book of nature! should the Christian find it less so? If man were not fallen, with what devout and lofty admiration, and with what profit, would he study it? If man had not fallen, this book of nature might have been the only religious writing he would have received, or needed. Or if a Bible had been written, how different would it have been, in its contents and its intents, from that we now have. A Bible given for a sinless earth—what a book must that have been!—with its revelation of God's will; its record of God's providence over such a world; man's history here and translation hence; its genealogies; its prophecies; its poetry and song; its silence as to a Redeemer!

Now childhood is the time to awaken this love of nature, and enforce its teachings. Then, when the world is fresh to us—fresh as our own existence, we are peculiarly susceptible to its purest and most happy influences. The love of nature is an instinct which God has given us. None are born without it. He designs that it be cultivated. But, neglected in infancy, it becomes perverted, dwarfed, or dormant—*lost* it never is, nor can be, wholly—as years and cares come on. You can make the *child* feel the poetry of nature—the religion and the poetry—you can make him sympathize with the beautiful and the grand, and feel the divinity that speaks in them; but such feeling, religious or poetic, you find it difficult to awaken in the adult bosom that has not cherished it from childhood. You can make the child see God in the dew, the flower, the zephyr, and the rainbow— in the slightest breathings and faintest foot-prints of his presence; while the grown-up, undevout in nature, will hardly apprehend him in the drought, the whirlwind, and the earthquake. It is of these, and not of the instructed child, that Thomson says:

> But wandering oft, with brute unconscious gaze,
> Man marks not Thee, marks not the mighty hand,
> That, ever busy, wheels the silent spheres.

Of the ways of *Providence*, also, my mother was an attentive observer, and accustomed us to be so. And is not this, too, an important part of parental duty? Is it not an essential means of forming a correct practical religious character? There is over and around us a wise, beneficent, *disciplinary* providence. It is minute and universal. Are not two sparrows sold for a farthing? and not one of them shall fall on the ground without your Father. But the very hairs of your head are all numbered. How important, then, is it, to recognize the fact and the methods of such a providence—habitually and reverently.

And where is that providence more manifest than over households; and where is the thought of it more affecting? How deep and tender is the interest God takes in the *family!*—the first institution that he formed on earth, and, so to speak, the last that he will neglect. And for obvious reasons. He knows that there our joys and griefs chiefly centre. There his dispensations reach us most directly and effectively; there he "purgeth" the grown plants, and nurses the seedlings of his church. I can feel that God is every where; I can recognize his hand in larger and in smaller events—in the steps of individuals and in the affairs of multitudes and nations, but I nowhere feel his presence as in the domestic circle —especially in the season of sickness and of sorrow. In that circle, therefore, is the fact of his providence to be specially recognized and taught.

The observance in question leads to gratitude and trust, to watchfulness and prayer, to hope, patience, and submission. It is eminently instructive. Who is so practically wise, so sustained and calm amidst the vicissitudes of life, so kept from wild and ruinous adventures, as is the man who best observes, and most implicitly obeys, the leadings of God's providence? Providence is history, and history is experience, and experience is wisdom. What is a large portion of the Bible itself but a record of God's providence? There we read it as such. But our own life and age are as full of that providence as were the lives and ages of the Bible, and we ought to read and understand it in the same light, and with the same reverence. The providence of God is a *current revelation*, daily, hourly, momentarily given, *intelligibly* given, most solemn in its nature, most momentous in its results, as it regards both our mortal and our immortal interests. Should not our "eyes be open and our ears attent" to such a book?

Childhood is the time for forming this habit, also. You can make the *child* recognize the providence of God in every thing—in every pulse of health, or of languor; in every realized or disappointed hope; in every danger and deliverance; in every joy, in every grief; but the habit is slow to form itself in later years. The adult unbeliever—negligent from childhood, and still negligent, lives on, obtuse to the most palpable facts of providence—regards not the work of the Lord, neither considers the operation of his hands.

CHAPTER XX.

Educational uses of Employment.—Practical Benevolence.—Incidents in Edinburgh.—Moral Influence of Love of Home.—Matrimony.—Religious Character of my Mother.—Filial Regrets.—Passion for the Sea.—Concluding Paragraphs.

ONE of the greatest wants of our nature, physical, mental, and moral, is *employment.* It is impossible that health, happiness, and virtue should exist without it. Now, the benefits of employment, whatever they are, may all be written down among its *educational* uses. There are, besides health and cheerfulness, various other qualities, such as patience, subordination, mental vigor, virtuous and kindly dispositions, which are hardly attainable without the aid of useful industry. I speak of *physical* employment. Studies must, of course, fill up a large share of the time of well-educated children; but mental labor alone is not sufficient; there should be manual labor also. To say nothing of the body's soundness, it is not study alone that makes the best scholars, and soundest minds, or the most amiable inmates of the family.

The educational uses of employment, of some kind, are as early, almost, as the child's existence. The infant that creeps across the carpet to reach an attractive object, not only exercises its limbs, but exercises its mind also; and the elder child that rocks or amuses the younger, is practicing a lesson at once of patience, usefulness, and duty. Employment is not only a most important, but an indispensable means of educating the *temper*. And this use it has, from infancy to manhood, and indeed, onwards, to life's end. My mother understood this. If we were restless, unhappy, *out of humor*, she would find something for us to *do*— not as a task, or a punishment, but from some welcome motive—ostensibly to serve and oblige her, it might be, but really to relieve and benefit us. I have observed her do the same with her grandchildren. When they were unhappy, and neither their mothers nor themselves knew what troubled them, she would simply find some means to occupy, and so to content them. It was *ennui* that ailed them; for infancy and childhood have their ennui, as all *amusement-seeking* people have

A child unemployed, habitually, or for the hour, can hardly be good-humored.

To visit and to watch with the sick, to go to the house of mourning, to assist the needy—all such charities she encouraged us to practice, as well as to give money for missionary and philanthropic purposes. She wished us to do so for our own sake, no less than for that of the objects of our kindnesses; feeling that the heart must be *exercised* in goodness, as well as taught by precept, or it will be sterile. Theory alone forms no habits, nor will the "luxury of doing good" be believed on hearsay merely.

It is attentions of the kind which I have mentioned that make the sympathizing and obliging neighbor; and it is this sort of benevolence that most adorns the Christian. It is such *personal* attentions, involving personal sacrifices, that most test the reality, and most promote the growth of benevolence in the heart, He that is free to render these, will not be backward to give of his money.

How beautiful is beneficence in a child, and how prognostic of the philanthropy of the man!

But it must be cultivated early, or selfishness, indigenous and rank, will overgrow the soil. I observed a little boy, of four or five years old, as he was entering one of the churches in Edinburgh, drop his heavy English penny into the plate at the door, for the benefit of the poor, with a simplicity and seriousness of manner that showed the act to be considerate and habitual. That act declared the character of the family that nurtured him, and assured me that in the age of philanthropy that was before him, if he lived, his heart would be full of its spirit, and his hand open to its claims. In the same city my attention was arrested by a very little child playing on the edge of a precipitous height, and in danger of instant destruction. I hastened to save it; and observing a young girl, about ten years old, strolling near, who told me she knew its parents, I desired her to lead it home. "It's nane o' my brither," she said, and walked away.

It was an important object with my mother, as being essential to the moral safety of her family, to make *home* pleasant. He that has no home-attachments, that is not happier there than elsewhere, is, for that reason, far more likely to be vicious. Every domestic tie, every domestic pleasure, is itself a virtuous feeling, and is a safeguard from vice. What are the elements of a happy home? Love, first of all, the soul of all—mutual love, conjugal, parental, filial, and fraternal—love, confidence, and harmony. There must also be neatness and order, and a measure of taste and refinement, even in the humblest dwelling, such as Christianity, if listened to, dictates and commends. There must be industry and mutual helpfulness; judicious reading, conversation, and innocent amusement. In such a home—if *piety* pervade, or, at least, preside over it, without which such a home can hardly be—all virtues have their most congenial soil, all pleasures their purest and most unfailing earthly source.

This subject suggests another. Next to religion, no concern is so important to the future happiness of children as the choice they will make of companions for life. Perhaps there is no subject on which parents seriously converse with them so little. It may be thought that advice on that subject will amount to little: love being so blind that it will choose as it will, in spite of counsel. I do not believe this. Marriage is a proper subject, at a proper time, for parental advice; which, if it be judiciously and timely given, may reasonably be expected to have a cautionary, if not a directive and decisive power. Or perhaps the reserve is owing to delicacy. In that case, there are always judicious books at our service.

However, our surest way is, so to educate the minds and manners of our children that their own tastes shall guide them. Intelligence will hardly ally itself to ignorance and dullness; nor refinement to coarseness and vulgarity; nor piety to ungodliness. My mother's chief concern for us, in this matter, was, that *piety* might be a *sine qua non* in our choice. If there be *piety, good sense,* and *good temper*, the rest are non-essentials.

But I may seem to you to forget that you have not proposed to me, as I have not to myself, to write a formal treatise; and a few lines or paragraphs more shall bring me to an end.

I think you will have perceived that the parent of whom I have been writing exerted a happy influence over her household. Her character as a Christian was eminently symmetrical, and her example shone with that uniform and quiet lustre that, together with her instructions, could not but be convincing. Those who lived most intimately with her were most impressed with the sincerity of her faith; while to others her light was not hid. An aged, pious mother, of the Baptist Church, had a son, a professional man, in middle life, who was somewhat skeptical. She mentioned to me that, in one of her conversations with him, expressing her earnest desire to see him a Christian—"I don't know about these Christians," he replied; "I don't see many of them." "But do you not see *any*, my son? For if there be so much as one, that one is an evidence of the reality of religion." "Yes mother, I can mention one; there is Mrs. —— [referring to my mother]. No one that knows her can doubt either the reality or the excellence of religion, as it appears in her." She could not live with others, or be much conversant with them, without endeavoring to promote their spiritual good. A number of those who lived with her as domestics, and especially several poor children whom she received in that capacity, some of whom were very untoward subjects when they came to her, became hopefully pious through her instrumentality.

HER CHEERFULNESS. 233

To me, taking her life through, including the more checkered portions of it, there is no feature of her piety more pleasant to contemplate than its serenity and *cheerfulness.* Perhaps there was none more persuasive. The natural heart is apt enough to regard religion as a gloomy sentiment, and it is well if its repugnancy be not aggravated by the sanctimonious and mortified demeanor of some of its professors. But I am happy to say that she who gave me my first ideas of religion impressed me with its cheerfulness. She herself was habitually cheerful, and it was evident that her religion made her so: it was in her a constant source of serenity and joy—a well of water springing up into everlasting life, refreshing her own spirit, and those about her.

If I have mixed up my own filial feelings with these recollections, it is because it was unavoidable; nor is my having done so irrelevant to my subject: for the feelings of the child are indicative, generally, of the character and influence of the parent. How much does the judicious Hooker tell us of the character of his mother in the following simple expression of filial feeling: "If I had no other reason and motive for being religious, I would earnestly strive to be so for the sake of my aged mother, that I might requite her care of me, and cause the widow's heart to sing for joy"— words which I can adopt in the fullness of their import. If, in a life filled with blessings, there be any one for which I can be thankful to God, it is, that he gave me a pious mother.

But what son or daughter can look back to the season of childhood and youth without filial regrets? I certainly loved my mother; I was not, I think, undutiful; yet my memory is not free from very sensible regrets on her account. I regret that I did not earlier and better appreciate and heed her counsels, on many subjects. I regret the years of deep solicitude, the anxieties and tears which my impenitence, and neglect of a Saviour, occasioned her. I have reason to remember that that concern was constant, and that it sometimes rose to strong crying and tears. In one of my absences from home for several months, though I was more than ordinarily impressed and thoughtful at the time of my leaving, I became uncommonly giddy and unreflecting. In every letter I wrote home she looked for some symptom of seriousness; and finding nothing but levity, she would go to a retired place, and pour out her heart to God, with weeping and supplication. Such solicitude my particular case occasioned her, and it was the same with regard to all her children. How much should I have spared her by an earlier devotion of myself to Christ!

I remember with regret another cause of uneasiness I gave her. There was a period lasting through half my boyhood, when I indulged a foolish inclination to the sea. My father was averse to it, but regarding it as a boy's transient dream, did not trouble himself much about it; only he would say occasionally, "It is a dog's life, and perilous to life and morals." But she, more aware of the force of my inclination—for it was a deep and growing passion, a *penchant*, and not a whim —set herself, with all a mother's power, to counteract it. Every instance of shipwreck and disaster she met with in the papers she would mark for my perusal. When the night was black, and thunders roared, and winds shook the house, she would say, What a night to be upon the water! Or when a snow-storm raged along the coast, she would say, How dreadful to the sailors: we shall hear of many a frozen limb, and many a crew lost! This did not move me. The very dangers of the sea have their attractions to young imaginations; and on the deep, too, as on the land, " all men think all men mortal but themselves." Her greatest hold was on my conscience, and my love for her; and it was well she had an *educated* conscience on which to operate.

She represented to me the *moral* dangers of the sea—that the sailor is away from all religious privileges—has no Sabbath—is beset with evil examples—mixed up with such as are profane, intemperate, lascivious (which used to be the character of sailors much more than now)—and that he is often overtaken by a death so sudden that he has no time to prepare for it. All this I listened to; it had its weight with me; I ceased to agitate the matter; and I can never be too thankful that a kind Providence, chiefly through her influence, kept me from a course, of which, had I once entered on it, I cannot tell what might have been the issues, spiritual or temporal.

Ignorance and low propensities, or an idle, roving disposition, no doubt, often incline a boy to be a sailor. But the inclination is not always to be attributed to such a cause. It is often coupled with intelligence, and is a love of enterprise, a desire to see the world, a love of sea sublimities, or sympathy with what is truly noble in the sailor's character; in proof of which are there not many of the finest hearts and intellects upon the deep? and he who reasons with the subject of it on the supposition that it springs from low and vulgar sentiments, reasons in the dark. The boy sees, too, only the brighter aspect of the matter, the holiday portion of the maritime life. How beautiful to *any* eye, and most of all to the romantic eye of boyhood, is a fine vessel, with her sails swelling in the breeze, upon a sun-lit water. How jovial the sailors coming home, and how rich in foreign wealth and luxuries. Of all men sailors seem to such an eye the lightest-hearted, and the most generous. And their life, what is it but a pastime—hoisting sails, steering, and singing O-heave-o! Who wonders that a young imagination should be captivated by a picture so illusive? Add to this, the more rational ideas of the seaman's usefulness, of office and command, and important trusts, of acquaintance with the world, gain, competence, and retirement, and our wonder will be still less.

It may have given you surprise that I have written, not, indeed, a memoir, but yet as though my subject were not living. I have done so because it has somehow suited my feelings to throw the shadows of remoteness over the period chiefly had in view, that of the education of her children, and because she is in fact as dead to the world, almost, as if she had gone to her rest long since. In the family of a daughter, far from the place of her former residence, she lives, as you know, in much infirmity, and in deep seclusion, surrounded by none of the scenes and associations, and none of the acquaintance, with which she used to be familiar. Her children, widely scattered, can visit her but seldom, and they feel at every parting that it is likely to be the last. One of them is "gone before;" in one of the states of the West his flesh rests in hope. Her mind is not sensibly decayed, but her bodily infirmities are great. She has, as you are aware, been quite blind for several years; and repeated casualties, in consequence of her blindness, have rendered her almost helpless now. Conversation has become difficult; so that, of external sources of enjoyment, she is in a great measure bereft. One of her severest trials is, that she can no more go to the house of God. To one of her natural activity what a privation must it be not to be able to walk, even so much as to feel her darksome way from one room to another, or along the cool piazza. But, with her love of reading, and her admiration of the face of nature, a greater affliction is the loss of sight. None but those of her tastes and habits, and in her condition, can appreciate those affecting lines of Milton :—

>   Thus with the year
> Seasons return; but not to me returns
> Day, or the sweet approach of even or of morn,
> Or sight of vernal bloom, or summer's rose,
> Or flocks, or herds, or human face divine;
> But cloud instead, and ever-during dark
> Surrounds me, from the cheerful ways of men
> Cut off, and for the book of knowledge fair
> Presented with a universal blank
> Of nature's works, to me expunged and ras'd,
> And wisdom at one entrance quite shut out.
> So much the rather thou, celestial Light,
> Shine inward, and the mind through all her powers
> Irradiate; there plant eyes, all mist from thence
> Purge and disperse, that I may see and tell
> Of things invisible to mortal sight.

That celestial Light does shine inward, and with a radiance that no earthly clouds can dim. She is a most edifying example of serenity and patience; having a desire to depart, and to be with Christ, which is far better, but yet, with cheerful submission, waiting God's will.

How often does God reserve for his children their severest outward trials to the closing period of their lives. And he seems to me to do this oftenest in the case of those who have been longest and most constant in his service. This may seem mysterious; to the skeptical and presumptuous it may look like desertion or forgetfulness, on his part. But his designs are ever wise and gracious, and his faithfulness reacheth to the clouds. It is thus that religion is exemplified in all circumstances, in all extremes; it is thus its sustaining power is manifested when nature sinks without it; it is thus that piety is fully ripened; and is it irrational to think that thus the saint's rest will be the sweeter when it comes, as sleep is sweeter after toil and pain; and that heaven will be the brighter from the contrast, as the morning is more brilliant that succeeds a starless night?

CHAPTER XXI.

The Old Homestead Revisited.—A Boy's Resolve.—Changes.—The Old Meeting-house.—Adventure on the River.—Trusting in Providence.—The Bethel Oak.—Bruin.—The Shady Mile.—Farewell.—Bruin's Death.

Not many months since, the author of this volume was able to gratify a long-deferred desire to revisit the home and scenes of his childhood. Ten years had passed since he had been in the place at all; and for many previous years his visits there had been but infrequent and flying ones. He wished once more to go over the entire old homestead, and about the parish, in the spirit of thoughtful retrospection and profitable revery.

He took a young son with him, a boy of twelve years. *He* went in the spirit of adventure and romance, as was natural to his years; but with a feeling, too, of sacred regard for the ancestral objects he was going to see.

There was none of the family there to receive the visitors; the last of them having left long since. Feeling like a pilgrim where once his home was, and every face and voice were familiar, the author proposed to find lodgings at the public house. But the hospitality of the place prevented this.

Several days were spent in the visit, rambling, looking, musing. Not in taking notes; there was no need. All that the pen could record, and much more, would be distinctly and indelibly imprinted on the memory itself.

Nor shall our pen now occupy the reader much with irrelevant details. So far as these brief paragraphs recall a mother's image, and a mother's influence, he will not deem them out of keeping with the volume to which they are a postscript.

For convenience' sake, we will resume the pronoun I, and will speak as familiarly and confidingly as though we were still addressing our friend, Mrs. ——, of the Preface.

Every part of the homestead farm, ample as it was, we roamed deliberately over. My young companion, J., kept commonly at my side; but was often running off to plunge into some mysterious dell, or to show himself upon some odd clump of rock, or airy hillock. What a luxury is young life! He had his ecstasies, I my musings; both, for the most part, in a quiet way. I dare say we sympathized, each with the other, in his emotions, however dissimilar, in most respects, might be the nature of our respective thoughts and feelings. Indeed, what was mine, for the time, but my own young life over again, without its bounding spirits, and shaded with the hues of later and more chastened days?

At the close of one such rapturous, romantic day, so full of historic interest, as well as of its own passing incident and adventure, as we turned, amid the shadows of a splendid sunset, to go to our lodgings, he said, emphatically and thoughtfully, "This is the happiest day I ever spent;" and expressed the grand resolve, so like a boy, to buy back the place, some day, and live there.

Parts of the homestead tract, particularly in the rear, appeared a little strange to me,— as if agrarian or profane hands had been at work to mar and dishonor it, instead of leaving it as nature had formed, and we had loved and left it. Huge stone fences had been run here and there, making divisions and subdivisions of the property into all shapes and sizes of lots, signifying that A had bought on this side, and B on that,— giving me a feeling of confinement and obstruction where once my range was large and free, and offending me with man-made deformities, where nature had cast the surface in her rude, but inimitable and permanently interesting moulds. Of most of its fine old embellishments the tract had been despoiled. Groves and single trees — great stately oaks and elms, that showed for miles around, and beeches worthy of Virgil's verse — had been cut down. And quarries had been opened, littering the earth about them with their vast unsightly rubbish — there to remain to the end of the world. It is wonderful how man can disfigure, as well as beautify, the earth.

But the larger features of the place were as they used to be, and as they ever will be; for man, with all his cupidity and digging, cannot do away with the everlasting hills, nor fill up the valleys. These, and the sparkling waters, were as I had seen them in my childhood,— these and much besides.

With every part of these diversified and picturesque grounds,— in connection with my young excursions there, through sights and sounds, through waterfalls and echoes, through haps and incidents, and in many ways,— my mother was, and will be, delightfully and *educationally* associated. The paths, and scenery, and animals, and birds, and wild-flowers, which she loved, with their teachings of Him that made them, I loved in sympathy with her, whether I also loved them naturally or not.

Of course these same localities and objects recalled the memory of my other parent, too; but in other, though interesting ways.

It was at the house in which I was born — the *Old* House, in distinction from the New — that my recollections naturally clustered most, and were earliest and most absorbing.

And, next to that, the venerable old "meeting-house;" whither at how early an age I was accustomed to be taken I cannot tell, but how constantly I well and gratefully remember.

And the road between the two, the winding green old road, shaded by trees and hill-sides, and sociable with babbling brooks; which also took us to the district-shool, and then, as we got old enough, to Littlepark Castle! There is nowhere a mile of road as rich in histories as that.

I felt grateful to the owner and occupant of the

old dwelling for the excellent condition in which he had preserved it. It lacked two years of being a century old. What an ancestral and home look it had! The amiable family permitted me to go wherever I wished, within or about it.

Through the front windows one looks down upon some five or more broad, winding miles of the Connecticut. Our farm fronted on that river, and was skirted at its sides, in part, by two tributary streams. How many of my boyhood hours were spent along its margin and on its surface, and how many in gazing at it by sunlight and moonlight! J. went quite down to it, not content to stop an inch short of it, and there stood a long time, meditating upon I know not what, and listening to the splash of cattle's feet wading along the other shore, just as his father had often done in his young days, when, as now, the air was still and the water glassy, and in a state to conduct the sound. The river here was said to be a mile wide; and yet I once heard, with perfect distinctness, across it, every syllable of a mother's voice, chiding her hurt child for its presumptuous climbing, and falling upon a rock.

A river is a tempting place to boys. Of various

ADVENTURE ON THE RIVER. 247

adventures on this, calculated to cause anxiety to parents, I will mention one, for the vigil which it cost my mother. In company with a boy of my own age, which might have been ten years, I went several miles down the river, on a great business of us boys, in a small skiff. We expected to be back early, but got delayed; and, when night came, were far from home, and, what was worse than night, began to be enveloped in thick, bewildering fog. It soon veiled the heavens impenetrably, and hid or mystified all sublunary things. It was impossible to see our way, and difficult, perhaps hazardous, to guess it. We crept along timidly, as near the shore as we could, feeling the flats with our oars; crossing at hazard soundless creeks' mouths and bays, running against piers and wears, nearly upsetting with the shock, and getting turned end for end as with a jerk or kick, or shot off beyond soundings and feeling-distance of the shore, by a strong current pouring round the mole we struck against,— often puzzling our wits to know which was fog, and which was land and water, and which was north, and not south.

The hour grew late, and we grew weary. My

fellow-voyager became disheartened, and at length despairing. He fancied we were going down stream; drifting fast and surely to the river's mouth, and out to sea, and so were lost! But, for myself, I remained quite composed and self-possessed, *trusting in Providence* — as I had been taught. We might be out all night; but God knew where we were, and would take care of us, and fetch us right in the morning.

That trust was of great value to me, then and often, as in crises of danger and alarm, such as the presence of a pestilence, or dreadful thunder, it sustained and calmed me. It was of great *moral* value, too, as it must be to every rightly-instructed child, not only as it led my thoughts to God, as being at once the author of perils and the only secure refuge from them, but also as there was coupled with it the reflection that sin, and a guilty conscience, are the only cause for fear in any case, under him. For the eyes of the Lord are over the righteous, and his ears are open to their prayers. And who is he that will harm you, if ye be followers of that which is good?

When, at length, the fog cleared away, as it did at midnight, we saw a light shining from a distant window. Whose it was we could not tell. But just then a dog barked, which I knew, by his voice, to be ours. Here we were, then, directly opposite to my father's. A strong flood-tide had, without our knowing it, borne us in the right direction. We pulled ashore, and ran home. I found my mother sitting alone, waiting for me, with the bright candle at the window. She was glad to see me, and heard my story, but said nothing of any uneasiness she had suffered on our account; at which I was a little surprised. Years after, alluding to this adventure, I asked her if she remembered it, and whether she did not feel anxious about us. "Yes, indeed!" was her reply.

Within my recollection, associated with that old house of my birth, there stood a tree, which I might have remembered only as a conspicuous object in a picture, or as a shady play-place, but for a circumstance which I have since known. It was a vast, symmetrical white-oak, a few hundred yards from the house; its lowest limbs drooping nearly to the ground, and forming a large area of dense, secluding shade. It has in my memory a mournful interest, when I think of some of the occasions which sent my mother there to pour out her full heart to God. There was a time, in the earlier part of her married life, when her too worldly father-in-law would come to the house on Sunday afternoons, after the family had returned from public worship, to plan business with his son for the morrow. This on the Lord's day! My father, no doubt, felt the impropriety of the thing, and was averse to it on his own account, as well as on his wife's; yet wanted the moral courage to disoblige his father by declining such consultations. My mother, distressed for them, and concerned for her children, some of whom were old enough to suffer from such an example, had no resource but prayer; and her Bethel Oak afforded her the needed seclusion. The Sunday consultations were discontinued. This piece of history I learned from her, incidentally, in conversation with her after she became blind.

How knowest thou, O wife, whether thou shalt save thy husband? At our father's grave I mourned afresh, and also rejoiced and thanked God for that instrumentality of a wife, through which, we trusted, he went to heaven.

If the reader has felt some kindly interest in

our early friend Bruin, as I trust he has, he will not be indifferent to a brief notice of him here. Indeed, but for such a notice, I should hardly have had an object in writing any of these notes.

I found him living in the same little wild, — grown *more* wild, it seemed to me, — whither he removed soon after he was married. Approaching the house, I noticed a small, switch-tailed, chestnut-colored horse standing at a post, which I recognized at once as an old acquaintance; having known him as a colt, under the *tutoring* of his master, a score of years before. The animal's age was twenty-three.

The wife was at the well drawing water. She gave me a cordial salutation. Her husband was not in the house, nor visible about it; but was "somewhere round, and would be there before a great while, she expected." I looked round, and there he was, within a few yards of me, dropped down, or coming, I could not tell whence, in his stealthy way, halting and looking askance, affecting not to know me; just as he used to come upon me when I was a child.

"Ah!" said I, "that long beard shows that you did not go to meeting, yesterday. I am sorry for that."

"I know it; I had to stay at home to keep folks' cattle from eating up my garden."

"They turn them into the streets, Sundays, do they?"

"Yes; and they're unruly; they hook down my fence."

"The more shame for them! to destroy their neighbors' crops, or keep them home from meeting!"

We went in. He and his wife were the only occupants of the house, their children being all married. The interview was not long,— the time, on my part, forbidding,— but was full of the interest of the past and present.

Thinking that this was probably the last visit I should ever make them, I wished it might be serious, as well as cheerful. He seemed touched at my allusions to the approach of death and the eternal world,— which could not be distant to a man of four-score years. His wife, who was pious (as some of their children are), freely responded to observations of that nature. He was silent, but, as I read his face and manner, thoughtful and pensive. No emotion would express itself in him in the way it ordinarily would in other people.

I bade him good-by at the house; but he proposed going with me as my pilot through a pathless thicket, to save circuitous travel, where he was sure I could not make my way alone. I did not need, but gratefully accepted, the service. He led the way, therefore, myself and son following, through bush and woods, and down and up. He seemed as agile, almost, as he ever was. His tones were full of kindness, such as come from hidden fountains. He inclined to talk but little. As we were traversing some wooded land of his, he bent down a beautiful young tree, and from its top cut a walking-stick for me,to be kept as a memorial of the visit; and, when I remonstrated with him a little for spoiling so fine and promising a tree, he quietly replied, "It's the cane I'm thinking of, and not the tree." How mistaken are they who look for the truest sentiment only where there is no rusticity!

In a deep glen, one of the wildest within my knowledge,— the *Shady Mile*, it might be called, — through which wound the road I was to take, my conductor stopped. We exchanged farewells repeatedly; and then, half hid in a bush, at the base and in the shade of the steep we had descended, he stood still and pensive, and followed us with his eye as far as the nature of the pass permitted, and then, sending another good-by to us down the dusky ravine, he glided into the bushes, and disappeared.

Farewell, my early and constant friend! May heaven be your home, at last! May I meet you there! Such was my mental adieu and prayer, as he vanished from my sight.

I resolved that, when I returned home, I would write him, earnestly and often, on the subject of his salvation. But, alas! procrastination! The next I heard of him, he was dead! Months had passed, and I had not so much as once written him,— though on the very day the news came I had definitely resolved to do so before another sun should rise and set. His age was eighty-two.

Other Related Solid Ground Titles

In addition to the volume which you hold in your hand, Solid Ground is honored to offer many other uncovered treasure, many for the first time in more than a century:

THE FAMILY AT HOME by Gorham Abbott
THE MOTHER AT HOME by John S.C. Abbott
THE CHILD AT HOME by John S.C. Abbott
SMALL TALKS ON BIG QUESTIONS by Helms and Kahler
MOTHERS OF THE WISE & GOOD by Jabez Burns
THE EXCELLENT WOMAN by Anne Pratt
OLD PATHS FOR LITTLE FEET by Carol Brandt
STEPPING HEAVENWARD by Elizabeth Prentiss
SHW Study Guide by Carson Kistner
THE YOUNG LADY'S GUIDE by Harvey Newcomb
WOMAN: *Her Mission and Her Life* by Adolphe Monod
THE KING'S HIGHWAY: *10 Commandments* by Richard Newton
HEROES OF THE REFORMATION by Richard Newton
HEROES OF THE EARLY CHURCH by Richard Newton
BIBLE PROMISES: *Lectures for the Young* by Richard Newton
BIBLE WARNINGS: *Lectures for the Young* by Richard Newton
THE SAFE COMPASS: *Lectures for Young* by Richard Newton
RAYS FROM THE SUN OF RIGHTEOUSNESS by R. Newton
LIFE OF JESUS CHRIST FOR THE YOUNG by R. Newton
FEED MY LAMBS: *Lectures to Children* by John Todd
TRUTH MADE SIMPLE: *Attributes of God for Children* John Todd
CHILD'S BOOK ON THE FALL by Thomas H. Gallaudet
CHILD'S BOOK ON REPENTANCE by Thomas H. Gallaudet
CHILD'S BOOK ON THE SABBATH by Horace Hooker

Call us Toll Free at 1-877-666-9469
Send us an e-mail at sgcb@charter.net
Visit us on line at solid-ground-books.com

www.ingramcontent.com/pod-product-compliance
Lightning Source LLC
Chambersburg PA
CBHW031138160426
43193CB00008B/178